Louis M. Seagull

SOUTHERN REPUBLICANISM

Schenkman Publishing Company, Inc.

Halsted Press Division

JOHN WILEY AND SONS

New York   London   Sydney   Toronto

for my MOTHER and FATHER
and RHEA

Copyright © 1975
Schenkman Publishing Company, Inc.
Cambridge, Massachusetts 02138

Distributed solely by Halsted Press, a Division
of John Wiley & Sons, Inc. New York.

Library of Congress Cataloging in Publication Data

Seagull, Louis M
  Southern Republicanism.

    "A Halsted Press book."
    Bibliography: p.
    1. Republican Party.   2. Southern States — Politics
and government — 1951-   I. Title
JK2357 1974.S4   329.6'00975   74-17381
ISBN 0-470-76875-4
ISBN 0-470-76876-2 (pbk.)

Printed in the United States of America

Contents

Chapter

iii

Preface

Great changes have been occurring in the American South in recent years. The revolution in civil rights, the economic development of the region, and the resurgence of serious inter-party competition are important dynamics of contemporary southern politics. Although they are inter-related, each is sufficiently broad to merit a separate study and it is the last of these—the resurgence of inter-party competition—which is the specific focus of the present work. In large measure, this study speaks to the relationship of social and political change.

Vigorous southern Republican competition is no longer a sometime feature of the American political scene, but the need to explain and interpret it as well as to account for its variation within the South is very much with us. Accordingly, this study presents an analysis of the character and stability of Republican electoral cleavages from the perspective of electoral realignment theory.

Inasmuch as this is a state-by-state analysis of aggregate voting and demographic data, measured at the county level, for a vast region, it will necessarily touch highlights and appropriate points of comparison at the expense of some detail. I hope that this approach will prove useful to those who would undertake more detailed analyses of change in the separate southern states as well as to those who would benefit from a general review and interpretation of recent southern Republicanism.

The central quest has been for a perspective applicable, in varying degree, throughout the region. My major argument is that there has been a realignment in the southern Republican vote, that its reliable basis is in the white collar sector, and that this finding rests consistent with the evolving New Deal electoral realignment.

It should be noted in the beginning that the 1972 presidential election did not conform to this pattern, thereby providing one manifestation of the highly unusual character of politics in that year. This is surely an exciting time to write about American politics but an exasperating one as well for those who would delineate with confidence future political patterns. Much has been written regarding the passing of the New Deal electoral alignment and its replacement by something else, usually not well specified. Of course this is possible, and I explore it where it seems to be plausible. However, I do not subscribe to the notion that the New Deal alignment is permanently in eclipse but rather I see the politics of movement and ephemeral tendencies as the occasional alternatives to this alignment. The politics of 1972 is just such an occasional alternative. Moreover, the meaning of the politics of 1972 for future political patterns may become all the more obscure given the Republican setbacks after the season of Watergate and economic distress. One thing that seems certain, however, is that in a period of Republican decline, the vote in the South will be reduced to its more usual base, which emerges clearly from the realignment perspective.

I am grateful to Alfred S. Schenkman for the opportunity to present these findings and argument. I also wish to acknowledge with appreciation William Ascher's careful reading of my exposition in Chapter II. I also benefited from the help of two student assistants, Dennis Curran and Jeffrey Gaster. I owe a special debt to my wife, Rhea, who patiently read and commented on several drafts of the manuscript, and whose skills as a professional journalist had an impact on the clarity and style of this work.

In its original form, this study was a doctoral dissertation in political science at the University of Chicago, completed in 1970 under the direction of Duncan MacRae, Jr. I remain grateful for his guidance, criticism, and, especially, his encouragement. I am also grateful to dissertation committee members Theodore J. Lowi - for his encouragement, his stimulating letters of criticism, and his exhortations to see beyond the data - and J. David Greenstone for his attention, direction, and criticisms. With such a committee, and in the environment of the University of Chicago, the dissertation experience was exciting and fulfilling. The manuscript has gone through considerable development in subsequent years as my own understanding of the dynamics of party and American politics has deepened, and as two additional general elections have transpired. Accordingly, and indeed, in any event, responsibility for whatever liabilities remain is mine alone.

Louis M. Seagull

Philadelphia, Pennsylvania

Chapter I

The Decline of the Democratic South

The recent political history of the American South is largely a story of resistance against federal authority and revolt against the national Democratic party. It is also the story of spectacular Republican party development. Indeed, in 1972 the term "solid South" meant a Republican South, at least for presidential voting, in direct opposition to the traditional sense of the term. The very large southern Republican pluralities in 1972 suggest the politics of a movement rather than that of stable social cleavage. It is too soon to determine whether this movement represents the wave of future politics in the South. However, it is possible to examine retrospectively the cleavages attending this spectacular Republican party development and to differentiate between durable and ephemeral ones. Now more than ever, this is an important task for the student of southern and American politics.

Since 1952, substantial Republican voting in the South has become commonplace. In the period from 1952 through 1960, serious Republican competition existed largely at the presidential level—hence the term presidential Republicanism. Since 1962, this competition has extended to nearly all gubernatorial and U.S. senatorial contests and to many congressional elections as well. The 1968 and 1972 presidential elections exemplified the decline of the formerly solidly Democratic South. In 1968, Democratic nominee Hubert Humphrey captured only one state, Texas, while Republican candidate Richard Nixon and third-party candidate George Wallace harvested the electoral votes of the remaining ten states of the former Confederacy. In terms of popular votes in the South, the Democratic nominee finished third in the three-way contest. In the Nixon landslide of 1972, the Republican President's popular vote pluralities in the southern states generally exceeded those outside the region. The last time the solid Democratic South was a reality was in 1944. Since then many southern votes have gone to non-national Democrats, be they Dixiecrats, Independents, American Independents, or Republicans. But the strength and distribution of these votes have been irregular. Moreover, the electoral revolution which is competitive southern Republicanism has affected the

1

southern Democratic parties and national presidential coalitions. Thus, change in one dimension of southern politics has important implications for all of American politics. Again, this warrants analysis of the cleavages underpinning Republican voting in the South.

Although the focus of this study is electoral change, it takes into account the social, economic, and racial revolutions in the South which set the context for this change. Electoral change itself is a general phenomenon with several analytically distinct dimensions. Accordingly, the actual size of the vote and the cleavages which produce it are two different matters. It is the latter which is the central focus of this study. In turn, these cleavages are viewed from the perspective of their newness as well as their stability.

Recent electoral change in the South gives rise to many questions. Perhaps the most basic of these is whether it is a durable change and what it might mean for the politics of the South and the nation. Even the most cursory review of the presidential elections since 1952 and of the gubernatorial and senatorial elections since 1962 indicates that the images, appeals, and bases of support of the candidates have been variable. It is the purpose of this analysis to delineate alternative patterns of Republican voting and to assess their durability. It is an inquiry into which of these patterns constitute a realignment, or durable change, of the social and political bases of the vote. This question, in turn, leads to probes of the mechanisms of change and the implications of such change for future American politics.

The One-Party South: Bases and Change

From the perspective of history, inter-party competition was not unknown in the American South. Prior to the Civil War and during the decades of the 1870's and 1880's, elections were quite competitive. This competition persisted in the period beyond the withdrawal of federal troops and the end of Reconstruction. Yet, between the 1890's and 1952, extreme loyalty to the Democratic party was by far the norm. Of course, there were geographic and temporal exceptions to this pattern. Throughout the entire period many mountain dwellers along the range of the southern Appalachians, from Virginia to Alabama, have been strongly Republican. In 1928 the revolt against Democratic presidential nominee Al Smith, on the part of otherwise loyal Democrats, yielded Republican victories at the presidential level throughout the rim South. Despite these exceptions, the election of 1896 marked the beginning of an era of sectional politics for the nation and no other region matched the South in terms of the intensity and duration of sectional loyalty.

The political expression of sectionalism was Democratic hegemony—the "solid South." Many forces underpinned this sectionalism but the major force was that of race and the cause of white supremacy. The emergence of the "solid South" coincided with the emergence of Jim Crow statutes across the region. This was more than mere coincidence. The solidarity which sectionalism compelled was necessary to disfranchise the Negro. [1] This most basic of supports for sectionalism has become increasingly untenable in recent decades, beginning with the U.S. Supreme Court's outlawing of the white primary election in its 1944 decision, *Smith v. Allwright*. A decade later the Supreme Court's *Brown v. Board of Education* decision declared unconstitutional racial segregation in the public schools. Major civil rights legislation in 1957, 1960, 1964, and 1965 completed the legal revolution in the southern caste system, thereby removing a major basis for the solidly Democratic South.

The major expression of southern sectionalism was Democratic loyalty, which in turn became itself a major force supporting continued sectionalism. One cannot understand the extreme convulsions of recent southern history without recognizing the social revolution which has taken place. The tradition of loyalty to the Democratic party was the key mechanism for the former defense of the region.

Democratic dominance was forged at the same time that the southern electorate underwent a severe constriction. Both are intimately related; the first was made possible by the second. The purpose of southern sectionalism was two-fold. Externally, it presented a common front for the region in its defense against the nation. Democratic hegemony was both an expression of southern sectionalism and the principal defender of it. In this way sectional cleavages in the different states could be expressed in the Democratic primary elections, but not in the general elections. The containment of conflict was the direct effect, therefore, of the constriction of the electorate. Such constriction facilitates the prediction and control of political conflicts.

The triggering mechanism for the constriction of the southern electorate around the turn of the twentieth century was a reaction by southern elites, the Bourbons, to the threat of Populism. To assert their leadership over poorer whites, they invoked the spectre of Negro domination. In addition, the not-too-distant memory of the Civil War defeat and subsequent Reconstruction facilitated the appeal to loyalty to the Democratic party and, of course, thereby, to the South. More than in the case of any other region, regional identity and consciousness is an important and enduring factor in the South.

Once formed, the one-party South was sustained in additional ways. As the Republican party became the spokesman of the industrializing Northeast, the Democrats voiced the interests of the agrarian and rural areas—i.e. the South and West. The needs of the emerging dominant interests of the Northeast in post Civil War America and those of the South and West diverged greatly, principally on the question of the tariff. An economic issue of great substance, therefore, contributed to the political sectionalism of the time. It is noteworthy that since World War II, and especially during the past few years, the position of the South on tariffs, especially regarding the textile industry, has been reversed completely.

The decline of southern sectionalism had external, national origins as well. Much of twentieth century American electoral politics can be understood in terms of the progressive breakdown of the sectionalism formed with the election of 1896, the national alignment pattern which produced extreme Republican hegemony in the North and extreme Democratic hegemony in the South. The return of inter-party competition in the South in the second half of the twentieth century continued the process of breaking down the sectional cleavages, a process which occurred elsewhere during the first half of the century, principally following the election of 1928.

The external origins of the "solid South" can be found in two principal factors. First, Populism, though based in the South and West, was very much a national problem for the established interests. Within the national context, the ascendancy of the southern conservative Democrats effectively isolated the western radicals and deprived the latter of their likely allies, the poorer whites and Negroes, thus insuring the national supremacy of the northern Republicans. [2] The price for Republican supremacy in the nation was Democratic hegemony in the South, thus consummating one of the more important political exchanges in American history.

The second external basis for southern sectionalism was national acquiescence in the principle of white supremacy. Indeed, suppression of the Negro could not have been possible without external as well as internal approval. Allan P. Sindler writes that the institutionalization of white supremacy in the southern states after the turn of the century was born out of national unconcern for the South both because this region was unnecessary to the new national Republican majority evident after the election of 1896, and because of national weariness over the difficult task of improving the life of the Negro.[3] In a series of decisions in the 1890's, the U.S. Supreme Court made possible the South's elaborate legal structure of segregation, thus encouraging the further institutionalization of white supremacy. Recent decisions of the Supreme Court, federal legislation, the evolving stance and appeal of the national Democratic party, and changing public opinion, all point to national rather than state sovereignty regarding the legal status of race relations. This national change is a major blow against the former rationale of a solidly Democratic South.

Had the recent demand for the inclusion of the Negro into the southern political system been sponsored solely by the Republicans, perhaps in the spirit of the radical Republicans of the Civil War era, its effects would not have been nearly so traumatic. To the contrary, however, the principal sponsor of the Negro's civil rights during the past third of a century has been the national Democratic party. It would be difficult to overstate the cross-pressure southerners experienced between their anathema to the Republican party, born out of their memories of the Civil War and Reconstruction and the party's identification with eastern business, and their revulsion to the national Democratic party's solicitation of the Negro. The support for the Dixiecrats of 1948, and afterwards the Independents, was one response to this conflict.

Just as the external sanctions for southern racism was a mighty prop for southern sectionalism, so also is national change on this question a blow against southern sectionalism. The transformation of the national Democratic party over the past four decades, together with Republican avoidance of the issue, is a major problem for those who would still assert the position of the southern white man within the context of the two-party system. Of course, what is fascinating and ironic about this national change is, as Dewey W. Grantham, Jr., points out, that "the role of the Democratic party as the guardian of southern solidarity and the role of the Republican party as the perennial threat to southern interests were reversed."[4] This reversal is important in comprehending a crucial question for the assessment of recent southern Republicanism. The recent rise of Republican competition in the South can be understood as both the product of the attenuation of several of the bulwarks of southern sectionalism and as the reassertion of sectional interest but in a new manner. South Carolina's Republican Senator Strom Thurmond exemplifies the latter. It is difficult to ignore his explanation of why he was a Dixiecrat in 1948 and a Republican in 1968. According to the Senator's statements during the 1968 presidential campaign, the contemporary South has an alternative within the two-party system which was not present previously. Senator Thurmond's strong support for Nixon in 1968 was an important factor in the President's southern convention delegate strength in the nomination quest as well as in his general election strength in the region.

Other bases for the region's former sectionalism are changing greatly as well—principally economic and population movement factors. One of the great transformations in the contemporary South is the post World War II urbanization and suburbanization of this formerly rural and agriculturally depressed region. Moreover, this new urbanization is not based on heavy industry as it was in the North, with the possible exception of textiles. Rather, southern urbanization has been oriented toward light, highly skilled industries and services. Here, the dynamic population group has been the white collar rather than the blue collar one, a fact of great importance in this study.

What is important about recent southern urbanism is its impact on the changing social structure of the region. The existence of cities in the South is not new. What is new, however, is that post World War II urbanism made cities no longer subservient to agricultural and rural interests. Previously, not only were the cities submissive to the needs of the agricultural sector but they were themselves dominated by elites who sustained an aristocratic social structure. In both respects, the southern city then was not a source of innovation. Leonard Reissman argues persuasively that the importance of this is that the southern city, and of course the South in general, "lacked a large middle class which is typically the initiator and instigator for social changes in its own behalf . . . Without the middle class, urbanization and all of the changes associated with that process had but little support in the South." [5]

Urbanization has had important consequences for the attenuation of southern sectionalism. The concomitant economic development of the region has introduced new issues and interests which are of wider scope than the single-minded issue of white supremacy. Furthermore, the new economic interests are likely beset with the same problems as elsewhere in the nation. Thus, urbanization and economic development have led to increased heterogeneity of the South. This development is important in two senses. First, it facilitates ties between the South and the rest of the nation. Secondly, heterogeneity itself, socially, ethnically, or economically, is a condition which supports inter-party competition. Above all, southern urbanization has served as a magnet attracting northerners as well as southern rural dwellers. Admittedly, this is a source of potential cleavage within the southern urban context itself. The northern migrants do not share the common southern consciousness and historic identity which has proved so important to southern sectionalism. Voting Republican is not a traumatic experience nor a crisis for these people. By contrast, the southern rural dweller who is attracted to the city carries with him his southern orientation.

The character and timing of southern urbanization has facilitated a conservative Republican outlook. The new industrialism in the South has stimulated political attitudes akin to those of the Northeast earlier in the twentieth century. Everett Carll Ladd, Jr. suggests a plausible consequence of this late economic development. "The South was the last region to industrialize, but after 1950 it was industrializing with a passion. Much of this new industrialism of the South behaved like industrialism three or four decades earlier in the Northeast: it was, for example, militantly anti-trade union, opposed to large-scale governmental intevention in social and economic life, and generally conservative." [6] This is important as a positive ideational basis for the emergence of competitive southern Republicanism.

The Growth of Southern Republican Competition

The return of inter-party competition is a result of the changes affecting southern sectionalism and its former bulwarks. Recent Republicanism is itself the most dramatic manifestation of these changes. In turn, whether Republican voting contributes to the process of breaking down the walls of sectionalism or is rather an expression of southern sectionalism in a different guise, there is no question but that the South has entered into the national political battle in a manner very different than hithertofore. And more clearly than in any of the previous elections, the 1972 election saw presidential Republicanism the standard of the southern white man. But, whether this represents party development or the surge of movement politics will depend upon the institutionalization of the cleavages of that year.

Although Warren G. Harding cracked the solid South and carried the state of Tennessee in 1920 and Herbert Hoover more seriously challenged the Democratic South by carrying five rim South states in 1928, Democratic hegemony generally prevailed prior to 1948. And with the exception of a few mountain Republican congressional districts, whatever challenge was mounted was confined to the presidential level. Despite the incursions of Harding and Hoover, Franklin D. Roosevelt was able to pull the South back into its traditionally Democratic mold. In part, this reflected the very dire economic condition of the South during the depression, not to speak of the regional depression which existed for a decade previous to the national economic disaster. And, quite simply, the South remained a separate regional entity and a mainstay of the Democratic presidential coalition.

Despite southern Democratic loyalty during the Roosevelt years, the seeds of future discontent were sprouting and taking nourishment. Ironically, the South, which was originally an important component of the Roosevelt coalition, began to turn away from the national Democrats in response to the course of the New Deal program. Recent southern Republicanism has its roots both in the reaction against the New Deal and in the national electoral cleavages cut by the New Deal realignment.

Since 1932, the New Deal electoral realignment has set the course of American electoral politics and much of the domestic agenda of politics. The opposition of section against section has declined and has been replaced by the opposition of class against class as well as urban versus rural and later, urban versus suburban groupings. Nationally, the Democrats have appealed successfully to minority groups and persons of lower economic status; conversely, the Republicans have appealed to majority groups and persons of higher economic status. In recent years, status politics concerns have joined the more narrowly economic dimensions of conflict, attenuating the latter and giving rise to speculation that the New Deal realignment is no longer an adequate organizing principle for present American politics.

During the evolution of the New Deal realignment, the national Democratic party shifted its constituency toward the urban North and minority groups, including the Negro. Concomitantly, the South began losing its influence in the national Democratic party. Formerly, influence over the selection of the Democratic presidential nominee and the content of the presidential platform were important resources for the defense of the sectional South. This defense was eliminated as early as 1936, with the abolition of the two-third rule for Democratic presidential nominations.

The shift in constituencies also changed the national relationship of the two political parties with each other. The force of numbers propelled the Democratic party into majority status and the Republicans into the minority. The poor and the minorities constituted a majority of the population then. The Democratic party set the agenda for debate on public policy. In this process the position of the South altered sharply from one of influence in national policy to one of being an object of national policy. The southerner is correct when he asserts that he has not changed but that his party has. The South's electoral impotence was never more painfully evident than in 1948 when the Dixiecrat movement could not deny re-election to President Truman in the four-way contest of that year.

The New Deal realignment did not emerge full-blown simultaneously in all sections of the country. Rather, it emerged in an evolutionary fashion, touching different sections and groups in the country at different times. Walter Dean Burnham writes that:

> On the state level, years had to pass before the conservative, old-line Democrats who were suddenly propelled to victory during the 1930's were replaced by leaders more in tune with the programs of the national party. Realignment of party organizations and followings along national lines did not spread into a number of states in the far North until the late 1940's and early 1950's. Similar realignment in the South, at least below the presidential level, has begun to have statewide ramifications only since 1960. [7]

One of the most important consequences of this realignment has been the nationalization of politics. This is possible because similar groups of people in different parts of the nation tended to respond to political issues and parties in the same manner. In this sense, the growth of class cleavages tends to undercut the persistence of regional opposition. More and more, therefore, the political parties tied together people of similar circumstances in different parts of the country.

Although the Democratic South strongly supported the New Deal at the outset, substantial opposition to the Roosevelt program emerged after the President's reelection. Antipathy to the New Deal by conservative southern senators and Roosevelt's subsequent efforts to purge his antagonists in the 1938 primary elections were indicative of the divergent paths taken by the southern and northern Democrats. According to James T. Patterson, congressional opposition to Roosevelt during the late 1930's was in response to the increasingly urban dimension of the New Deal program then. "From the largely southern-western party of 1933," writes Patterson, "the Democratic party had become a coalition in which northern urban elements dominated." [8] From 1936 on, southern conservative opposition to the New Deal was increasingly a rural phenomenon; rural southerners were more conservative than urban southerners on economic issues.[9] Thus, at an early point, the urban dimension of the class cleavage was manifest. Throughout the period of Roosevelt's presidency, however, race issues were not part of the conflict.

Southern Democratic disaffection for the candidate as well as the program of the national Democrats exploded in the revolt of 1948, when a majority of the voters in four southern states supported J. Strom Thurmond and the States' Rights party - the Dixiecrats. Several features of this 1948 revolt are worthy of notice. First it was an immediate response to the national Democratic party's denial of complete southern autonomy over race relations. In 1947 President Truman's Committee on Civil Rights recommended the protection of the civil rights of minorities. [10] The President then urged congressional enactment of only some of the committee's proposals. Nevertheless, on the symbolic level, the South clearly perceived the threat. The changing stance of the national Democratic party on the issues of race was revealed in the Democratic national convention of 1948 which adopted a much stronger civil rights platform plank than had been proposed by the platform committee. This precipitated the exit of the Mississippi delegates and half the Alabama delegates from the convention and led directly to the States' Rights campaign of that year. [11] Clearly, then, while relations between the national Democratic party and the conservative southern Democrats had been less than the best since the period of the latter 1930's, it was the explosive issue of race which served to enflame the smoldering resentment of the South.

A second feature of the 1948 revolt is that the disavowal of the national Democratic ticket was not a repudiation of the various Democratic parties in the separate states. The Dixiecrats gained their electoral votes only in states where they preempted the names of the national Democratic nominees on the ballot with their own candidates. For example, Thurmond was the presidential candidate of the regular Democratic party of Alabama in that state, as was George Wallace in 1968.

In a more general sense, the revolt of 1948 was a response to the changing constituency of the national Democratic party. The very goal of the southern rebels - to show the national Democrats that they could not win the White House without the support of the South - speaks to the importance of this factor. The genesis of this idea may be found in the action of the Mississippi Democratic convention in 1944 which placed uninstructed electors on the ballot in the hope of introducing bargaining agents into the electoral college.[12] In subsequent years the notion of independent and bargaining presidential electors from the South received increasing attention. And, of course, the notion that the South could hold the balance of power in a deadlocked electoral college was most seriously and most successfully pursued in the American Independent party's campaign of 1968. It is likely that the hostility of the southern elites to the national Democrats in 1948 also reflected their realization of their hollow victory of 1944 - in which conservatives succeeded in denying the Democratic vice-presidential nomination to the incumbent, Henry Wallace, and instead agreed to substitute a border state moderate - Harry Truman.

During the period 1932-1948, therefore, there were fissures between southern and national Democrats and there was a major bolt away from the national party, but the disaffection did not then produce strong support for Republican presidential nominees, although the number of ballots for these nominees rose since the nadir of 1936. The Republicans in these states were a force apart from these conflicts and generally represented three different types of Republican partisans - the "post office" or patronage Republicans, Negro Republicans, and the hill Republicans. Aside from a few locally competitive mountain districts, the dominant form of Republican party organization was of the "post-office" type rather than the office-seeking variety. The sights of these Republicans were fixed on the quadrennial nominating conventions which they attended, generally supporting Senator Taft in the Republican presidential nominating battles of the 1940's, and on the patronage which a national Republican victory would yield them. They were relatively unconcerned with state politics and winning elections. And, of course, the smaller and less active that these Republican parties were, the more patronage the party activists could control for themselves following a national Republican victory. They had a real stake in a limited and non-aggressive Republicanism.

V.O. Key, Jr. aptly characterized the nature of southern Republicanism in this period. "It wavers," he said, "somewhat between an esoteric cult on the order of a lodge and a conspiracy for plunder in accord with the accepted customs of our politics. Its exact position on the cult-conspiracy scale varies from place to place and from time to time."[13] In all fairness to these political curios of Dixie, their ambitions and the political realities in the South were well matched. The importance of these organizations in this tale of southern Republicanism is that they were the antithesis of what serious inter-party competition demands. And when serious Republican competition did emerge in the South, especially in the deep South, it was in spite of and independent of these traditional organizations.

Simultaneous large-scale defections from the national Democratic party and Republican party growth did not occur until 1952. In that year support for Eisenhower came from the urban areas and the black belt[14] in addition to the traditionally Republican highlands.[15] Virginia, Tennessee, Florida and Texas—all rim South states—were carried by the Republicans.

Urban support for Eisenhower in 1952 was the first strong political indicator of economic and social change in the South. Moreover, this particular basis of Republican support was part of a phenomenon of national scope. Louis Harris asserts that Eisenhower was more popular among the white collar class than among any other group in the nation. He continues that:

> Over one out of every two white-collar voters in the South broke with a solid Democratic past and voted Republican. The shift was so decisive and so dramatic that in the end the white-collar people in the South voted nearly as overwhelmingly Republican as their counterparts in the North.[16]

Southern urbanism was white collar urbanism. And this white collar Republicanism became the most stable component of the new southern Republican vote. By contrast, the black belt Republicanism which emerged in 1952 proved to be an unstable source of Republican votes and did not support a Republican presidential candidate again until 1964.

The Republican party organizations in the South were not untouched by these changes in the mass electorate. In general, southern Republicanism, in its vote-seeking stage, has benefited from the infusion of two streams of partisans into the local organizations. The first stream was in response to the prospect of the Eisenhower candidacy, the second, in response to the prospect of Senator Barry Goldwater's nomination in 1964. Including the post-office Republicans, therefore, it is possible to identify three generations of southern Republican leadership during this period.

The pre-convention Eisenhower candidacy in 1952 represented a major challenge to the more traditional post-office Republican party organizations. Eisenhower partisans swamped the local caucuses and state conventions and elected Eisenhower delegates instead of Taft supporters to the national convention. Stephen Hess and David S. Broder write that:

> In Louisiana, Georgia, and, most notably, Texas, thousands of new recruits, almost all of them nominal Democrats, were sent swarming into precinct, county and state conventions to vote for Eisenhower delegates. The uproar and the battle continued right onto the floor of the national convention in Chicago, where the contested delegates were finally resolved in Eisenhower's favor, thus sealing his nomination. [17]

These new urban Republican organizational stalwarts, the successors to the post-office Republicans, themselves became vulnerable to assaults by the Goldwater partisans in the early 1960's.

White collar support for Eisenhower in the close nomination battle of 1952 was even greater in the general election. Harris suggests that the two features of his candidacy which were particularly attractive to white collar voters were his non-partisan stance and his internationalism. Similarly, this group had tended to support Dewey over Truman in the previous general election since the former, too, represented the modern wing of his party and did not stress partisan and economic divisions, as Truman did. [18]

Although the Eisenhower candidacy stimulated pre-convention citizen interest throughout the South, as it did in the nation, it should not be forgotten that the antipathy to the Democratic presidential nominee, Adlai Stevenson, on the part of prominent southern Democratic leaders produced another stream of support for Eisenhower. Governors Allan Shivers of Texas and Robert F. Kennon of Louisiana led "Democrats for Eisenhower" movements in their states. Governor James F. Byrnes of South Carolina led an Independent elector slate in Eisenhower's behalf in his state. Between the regular Republican slate and the Independent slate, the Eisenhower forces nearly accumulated a majority in South Carolina in 1952. Virginia's Senator Harry F. Byrd was officially neutral and unofficially disposed to Eisenhower. The Senator's position provided a sure clue to his followers. Two decades later, when another prominent southerner, John Connally of Texas, headed "Democrats for Nixon," he was acting within a well established tradition.

Race was not an issue of particular concern to the leadership generation which ousted the older Taft leadership in the southern Republican parties in 1952. This was, of course, the period before the U.S. Supreme Court's decision in favor of school desegregation. In contrast, southern militancy in defense of the institution of segregation came to have a great effect upon the Republican party organizations in the South during the early 1960's, when much of the second generation Republican leadership in the South was toppled by Goldwater partisans.

The early 1960's witnessed a new surge of citizen participation in Republican party organizations. Newly interested Republicans swelled the ranks of Republican activists and replaced the more moderate Republican leadership in several of these states, just as the incumbents had replaced the post-office Republicans in 1952. The Republican parties in Dixie were in a position, thereby, to contribute significantly to Senator Goldwater's first ballot presidential nomination in 1964. What is distinct about this third generation of leadership, however, was that many of these men were staunch Democrats of the conservative and racist stripe immediately prior to their conversions.

The changed emphasis of the southern Republican leadership in the early 1960's was in response to renewed efforts on behalf of the civil rights of Negroes by the federal executive branch. By that time, the major challenge to the South's traditional position on race had gone through a sequence of arenas—first in the Democratic party itself, as at its 1948 national convention, secondly through the U.S. Supreme Court in the 1954 decision against public school segregation, and finally in the incumbent national Democratic administration of the early 1960's. After a period of initial hesitation the Kennedy administration took a stand in this direction. This as well as the prospect of a Kennedy-Goldwater presidential contest served as a catalyst for many southern conservatives to abandon their habitual party and embrace Republicanism - at least on the presidential level. Obviously, the imperatives for this step were less compelling during the period of Eisenhower's presidency when the future leadership and appeal of the Democratic party were yet to be resolved. The stance of the Kennedy administration represented yet another defeat for the white South, within its traditional party, which reinforced the sense of defeat within the nation which the South experienced for a century.

It is clear that southern Republican development in the 1960's was a phenomenon of southern whites. The civil rights legislation of this decade made possible a massive transformation of the southern electorate; hundreds of thousands of Negroes finally entered the electorate, as Democrats. This hastened the development of lily-white Republicanism. Obviously, it also affected the stance and appeal of the Democratic parties. By 1970 the former stridency of the race issue in southern state house politics had been ameliorated and newly elected Democratic governors sought an accomodation with this electorate. A basic transformation in the structure of southern politics had occurred.

Since 1952, therefore, aggressive, vote-seeking Republicanism has been part of the new southern politics. But this Republican vote has represented different forces at different times and, indeed, sometimes at the same time. It is also true that the question of the salience of the race issue has been central to these alternative forces. The thesis of declining sectionalism is premised on the notion that with the attenuation of race as *the* issue of politics, political cleavages based on other concerns would emerge. This is an underlying theme of Key's *Southern Politics*. The thesis of increased and militant sectionalism, of course, turns on the notion that disaffection from the Democrats on the issue of race has led to increased Republican voting, as the only viable alternative. However, throughout the period since 1948, there have been alternatives to either political party — the Independents. The existence of these alternative forces finds reflection in the several "southern strategies" of recent years. Although the most clearly defined of these was Goldwater's 1964 strategy, the Nixon campaign of 1968 contained a recognizable southern strategy of a slightly different sort. Here the strategy was keyed largely to the rim South states, rather than to all of the South. No doubt the vigor of Wallace's campaign and the Alabamian's early strong showing in the polls compelled this shift. Nevertheless, the very existence of a three-way contest in 1968, in particular the Wallace appeal, pinpointed the distinction between exclusively racial and traditional forces and the broader and likely more durable force of white collar Republicanism.

The recently popular notion of a "southern strategy" reflects the historic problem of the stance of the national Republican party in regard to political discontent in the South and the possible opportunity for Republican advances because of it. Earlier in the twentieth century the problem was one of how to appeal to whites without alienating Negro Republicans, who were important in presidential nomination politics.[19] Early southern Republican strategies failed, in part because they were too transparent and compromising, and in part because the tradition of Democratic loyalty was too strongly entrenched. Quite simply, there was not yet reason to repudiate this tradition.

Previous to the Goldwater nomination in 1964, the southern strategy had been largely a vague but innocuous sympathy for the South on the part of national Republican candidates. Campaigning on the state house steps in South Carolina in 1952, Eisenhower stood up when the band played "'Dixie," declaring that "I always stand up when they play that song."[20] The strategy of sympathy was repeated in the early years of the Nixon presidency in the form of federal appointments, especially ill-fated Supreme Court nominations, which seemed designed to assuage the South's feeling of discrimination and victimization by the federal government.

The most explicit concept of a southern strategy is associated with the 1964 Goldwater campaign. Its uniqueness was its exclusionary character. In the words of Senator Goldwater, ". . . we ought to go hunting where the ducks are."[21] A 1963 article by William Rusher in the *National Review* elaborated the theory.[22] Rusher argued that the Republicans should forget about carrying New York and California and strike a conservative pose for the surer win in the South, which together with the usually Republican states of the Mid-West and mountain regions, could produce a national Republican plurality.

The exclusionary southern strategy, which was really a minimum coalition strategy, did not work. The 1964 election demonstrated that a regional appeal which exists at the expense of a national electoral strategy does not win a national election. This mistake is not likely to be repeated. The passage of time had rendered unnecessary an exclusive southern strategy. The nationalization of the issues of race—epitomised in the school busing controversy of 1972—together with the Republican presidential landslide in 1972, points to the utility of a national strategy which speaks to the concerns of most Americans, North and South.

Electoral Realignment

The question of the durability of recent southern Republicanism compels viewing it from the perspective of electoral realignment theory. The question of the meaning of recent voting change in the South compels attention to national electoral change. For now, as in the past, southern politics takes on meaning within the context of national politics.

V.O. Key, Jr. brought our attention to that form of electoral change which he termed an electoral realignment and which is heralded by a critical election.[23] A critical election, Key asserted, was one in which the depth and intensity of electoral involvement are high, the bases of the vote shift massively, and most importantly, this new electoral pattern is institutionalized in succeeding elections. It is this last attribute, the institutionalization of the new pattern which is the essential capstone of electoral realignment. It is important to emphasize that, within the context of Key's original formulation, a sharp shift in the basis of the vote can be considered a critical election only to the extent that its pattern persists in subsequent elections. Otherwise, it is merely an electoral departure and nothing more. A strict application of this theory, as originally formulated, has great relevance for appraising southern Republicanism in its 1964 and 1972 manifestations.

Since the publication of Key's seminal article, analysts have extended considerably our understanding of electoral realignment. This work was stimulated in part by Key's incisive beginning and in part by a realization that not all the attributes Key associated with realignment were maintained in time. Our understanding of realignment was elaborated and refined. Duncan MacRae, Jr. and James A. Meldrum contributed the notion of a critical election period rather than a single discrete critical election. They also highlighted the contribution of third-parties as "halfway houses" for those who were breaking with old partisan habits but were not yet moored in their new partisan homes.[24] For example, the Progressives of 1924 were supported largely by former Republicans who were later to support Roosevelt in 1932. At the same time the authors of *The American Voter* suggested a typology of elections which added the concepts of maintaining and deviating elections to Key's realigning elections.[25] Gerald M. Pomper later critiqued this typology by arguing that it was built upon two different dimensions not clearly distinguished—victory or defeat for the majority party and continuity or change of the underlying electoral cleavages.[26] He contributed the notion of a fourth type of election, a converting one, in which there is a shift in the bases of the vote but one in which the majority party retains its position in the electorate. He further suggested that electoral realignments need not occur with periodic regularity, as had been the conventional wisdom in the period following Key's original article.

Pomper's twin contributions are especially relevant to an assessment of contemporary electoral trends. Key originally noticed that past electoral alignments were bounded in time, lasting between three and four decades and that they represented the ascendancy and descendancy of groups, interests, and issues.[27] The combination of these two notions has confused analysis in recent years. Kevin P. Phillips' *The Emerging Republican Majority* is a case in point.[28] Phillips assumes that American alignment eras are temporally bounded and foresees the possibility that a new era is emergent which may persist until the end of the twentieth century which, conveniently, is some three decades away. The equation of a new majority era with a new electoral alignment is directly consistent with Key's original presumption. However, it is an unfortunate fallacy to confuse the size of the vote with the quality of the vote, or its underlying character of cleavage. Quite simply, a possible emerging Republican majority need not be inconsistent with the continuation of the New Deal electoral alignment, if the underlying cleavages do not shift. In this regard it is helpful to distinguish between the Roosevelt coalition, which included the South, and which produced a Democratic majority, and the New Deal electoral alignment itself, which does not necessarily predict a regional political configuration nor the majority or minority status for either political party. Indeed, from the perspective of cleavages alone, it is possible that the Nixon landslide of 1972, spectacular as it was, could prove consistent with the New Deal electoral realignment.

The concept of electoral realignment is important to the analysis of recent southern Republicanism because it serves to differentiate emphemeral or unstable change from that which is more durable. By definition, electoral realignment is a durable change in the social basis of the vote. The following chapters explore the durability of recent change by means of correlation and regression analyses. There remains still, however, the need to identify the mechanisms of electoral realignment.

Two general mechanisms, not necessarily in combination, antecede a durable shift in the vote. In addition to the critical election or critical election period mentioned above, there is the phenomenon of secular realignment. Both may be viewed as transmission mechanisms and important conditions for electoral realignment. Secular realignment refers to the gradual change in the composition of the population in terms of any given trait, together with the increasing political homogeneity or outlook of the group defined. Questions of population movement and the press of events upon different groups in the population are important here. V.O. Key, Jr. and Frank Munger's description of the sources of traditional political loyalties in Indiana exemplifies the phenomenon of secular realignment.[29]

The post World War II movement of northerners, often Republicans, into certain areas of the South, primarily the boom and retirement sectors of Florida and Texas, also constitutes one type of secular realignment. Attention to these long-term changes can yield clues to an impending electoral realignment. Thus, Democratic inroads in the urban and Catholic North in 1928 presaged the New Deal electoral realignment which was more sharply registered with the critical election of 1932.

A critical election is the second major mechanism of realignment. This refers to a sudden, massive dislocation of the vote. Essentially, a critical election involves the development of consciousness or, indeed, a shift in political consciousness, on the part of one or several segments of the population. The reshuffling of voting groups which is captured by a critical election then serves to define the contours of a new political era—at least until the advent of a new period of realignment.[30]

The evolution of the New Deal electoral and party realignment set the context for the realignment in the South. The southern response to the national Democratic party's increasing attention to its northern liberal constituency is one indication of this. Another manifestation of this context is the extension of inter-party competition into the South along the same lines of cleavage as elsewhere in the nation. The first response corresponds more directly to the stream of white racial protest while the second reflects the economically based realignment. However, although the term economic or class cleavage provides a handy way of referring to this phenomenon, the white collar basis of southern Republican voting will be considered in a sense broader than the narrowly economic.

FOOTNOTES

1. Donald R. Matthews and James W. Prothro, *Negroes and the New Southern Politics* (New York: Harcourt, Brace & World, 1966), p. 14.

2. An excellent discussion of the "system of '96" can be found in Chapter V of E.E. Schattschneider, *The Semi-Sovereign People* (New York: Holt, Rinehart and Winston, 1960).

3. Allan P. Sindler, "The South in Political Transition," in John C. McKinney and Edgar T. Thompson, (eds.), *The South in Continuity and Change* (Durham, N.C.: Duke University Press, 1965), p. 299.

4. Dewey W. Grantham, Jr., (ed.), *The South and the Sectional Image* (New York: Harper & Row, 1967), p. 55.

5. Leonard Reissman, "Urbanization in the South," in John C. McKinney and Edgar T. Thompson, (eds.), *The South in Continuity and Change,* pp. 81-82.

6. Everett Carll Ladd, Jr., *American Political Parties* (New York: Norton, 1970), p. 295.

7. William Nisbet Chambers and Walter Dean Burnham, (eds.), *The American Party Systems* (New York: Oxford University Press, 1967), p. 302.

8. James T. Patterson, *Congressional Conservatism and the New Deal* (Lexington, Ky.: University of Kentucky Press, 1967), pp. 333-334.

9. *Ibid.,* p. 331.

10. V.O. Key, Jr., *Southern Politics* (New York: Knopf, 1949), p. 330.

11. Ladd, *American Political Parties,* pp. 215-216.

12. *Ibid.*

13. Key, *Southern Politics,* p. 277.

14. The term black belt refers to areas of black soil, which were also the location of the former plantation economy and which still contained sizeable Negro populations.

15. The traditionally Republican highlands in the southern states are areas which never developed a plantation economy and hence were unsympathetic to southern secession in the Civil War.

16. Louis Harris, *Is There a Republican Majority?* (New York: Harper and Brothers, 1954), p. 134.

17. Stephen Hess and David S. Broader, *The Republican Establishment* (New York: Harper and Row, 1967), p. 332.

18. Harris, *Republican Majority*, pp. 127-128.

19. George Brown Tindall, *The Disruption of The Solid South* (Athens, Ga.: University of Georgia Press, 1972), p. 18.

20. *Ibid.*, p. 51.

21. *Ibid.*, p. 60.

22. *National Review* (February 12, 1963), pp. 109-112.

23. V.O. Key, Jr., "A Theory of Critical Elections," *Journal of Politics*, XVII (Feb. 1955), pp. 3-18.

24. Duncan MacRae, Jr. and James A. Meldrum, "Critical Elections in Illinois: 1888-1958," *American Political Science Review*, LIV (September, 1960), pp. 669-683.

25. Angus Campbell, *et. al., The American Voter* (New York: Wiley, 1960), pp. 531-538.

26. Gerald M. Pomper, "Classification of Presidential Elections," *Journal of Politics* XXIX (August, 1967), pp. 535-566.

27. V.O. Key, Jr., "Secular Realignment and the Party System," *Journal of Politics* XXI (May, 1959), pp. 198-212.

28. Kevin P. Phillips, *The Emerging Republican Majority* (New Rochelle, N.Y.: Arlington House, 1969).

29. V.O. Key, Jr. and Frank Munger, "Social Determinism and Electoral Decision: The Case of Indiana," in Eugene Burdick and Arthur J. Brodbeck, *American Voting Behavior* (New York: Free Press, 1959), pp. 281-299.

30. Undoubtedly Walter Dean Burnham's *Critical Elections and the Mainsprings of American Politics* (New York: W. W. Norton, 1970) is a major and provocative statement on realignment theory. However, it stands apart from the dominant tradition in realignment theory because of its focus on "critical realignment," a hybrid phenomenon which fuses together unusual sudden change and durable change. The usefulness of this concept is limited because not every massive alteration of the vote need lead to a realignment and not every realignment is produced by a sudden massive shift in the basis of the vote.

Chapter II

Analyzing Southern Electoral Change

The quest for the durable southern Republican vote compels a comparative analysis of this vote and its cleavages over time and across the southern states. Thus, the vote in presidential elections from 1940 to 1972 is examined in chapters III and IV in relation to three variables in each of the southern states. Chapter III deals with the states of the deep South—Alabama, Georgia, Louisiana, Mississippi, and South Carolina; chapter IV pursues the cleavages in the remaining states, those of the rim South. The distinction between the deep South and the rim South is a well established and useful one. It serves as a major organizing principle for this book. This distinction is not a mere arbitrary one, however, as factors of political history, population composition, and political response differentiate the two.

The past politics of the South has fascinated scholars and commentators because, in general relief, it seemed to stand apart from that of the rest of the nation. At the same time, the diversity within this vast region has not gone unnoticed. Thus, in southern politics, as in music, there is a pattern of theme and variations. This design has been pursued in the two landmark works on southern politics. In V.O. Key, Jr.'s *Southern Politics* there is a continuing tension between what is common throughout the South and what is variable across the states of this region. Writing at mid-century, Key approached the South through a detailed state by state analysis of the character of the Democratic party organizations and personalities and of the appeals of the different political protagonists. More recently, *The Changing Politics of the South* edited by William C. Havard, has provided a comprehensive account of southern politics in the period following that analyzed by Key and has continued to focus on the South through analysis of the separate states.[1] This latter work emphasizes the diversity of the southern experience and response.

The present study of southern Republicanism also proceeds in a state by state analysis of the eleven states of the former Confederacy, but in a more focused manner than the earlier more comprehensive accounts of southern politics. The present work views the Republican vote in the separate states from the perspective of a common set of cleavages. A major purpose of the present chapter is to introduce the variables which represent these cleavages. Necessarily, this perspective emphasizes what is similar as opposed to what is not. At the same time, this perspective reveals sharply variations which do exist. Thus, chapter IV will reveal that at times Arkansas and Florida have resembled the states of the deep South more than those of the rim South, the sub-region to which they are usually classified.

In casting this study at the aggregate level of analysis certain advantages and disadvantages should be noted, the choice of methodology and data always providing a constraint for analysis and interpretation. In this case, measurement at the county level and the explanation of the aggregate vote instead of party identification, preclude speaking of change at the individual level or underlying partisan loyalties. This refers to "ecological fallacy," or the problem of inferring individual level correlations from ecological or aggregative measures and relationships.[2] However, it is possible to analyze change in terms of aggregate contexts or sectors, such as the white collar sector. Moreover, the ready supply of county level voting and demographic data satisfy the need to study cleavages over time and for small sub-units in the region, such as states and sectors within states.

Variables and Contexts

In the following chapters the state Republican vote is examined in terms of the varying contributions to it of three different variables. These principal independent variables are the traditionally Republican, black belt, and white collar ones. They are measured, respectively, by the proportion Republican for President in 1940, the proportion Negro in the population in 1960, and the proportion of the employed population working in white collar occupations in 1960. All are county level proportions.

The first variable, the proportion Republican for President in 1940, serves two purposes. It separates the newer from the more traditional Republican vote, through the technique of controlling the 1940 vote. At the same time it permits a comparison of the effects of the traditionally Republican vote, across the states, upon the newer Republican votes as well as a comparison with other bases for the vote. By far the major portion of the traditionally Republican sector was composed of the mountain

Republicans of the southern Appalachians. There were exceptions to this, however, and they will be noted where appropriate.

The 1940 Republican vote is a measure of traditional Republicanism because it measures Republican voting at its nadir, prior to the changes introduced by the Second World War and post-war decades. While the war did distort voting patterns and lead to lessened Democratic strength in certain midwestern counties,[3] the South was unaffected by these tendencies. If anything, the South was pro-British and internationalist in outlook, given its relative lack of non-British ethnic groups, its historical affinity for Britain, and its military tradition.

The second variable, the proportion Negro in 1960, measures a phenomenon of great importance in southern history and politics, as is always recognized. For the purpose of convenience, this variable is termed the black belt. Strictly speaking, however, the black belt refers to areas of black soil, which were the plantation areas of the ante-bellum South and which yet contain high concentrations of Negroes in the South. Prior to the mid-1960's, it was safe to assume that the electoral behavior of the black belt was almost entirely the expression of white voters. Since the passage of the Voting Rights Act of 1965, however, this is no longer the case, which is a source of difficulty in aggregate analysis. Thus, where available, data on Negro voting registration rates are also included in the analysis, in order to control their effects on the other independent variables.

The third variable, the proportion white collar, is defined by the U.S. Census Bureau as including:

> professional, technical and kindred workers, managers, officials and proprietors, except farm, clerical and kindred workers, sales workers.[4]

Thus, this variable refers to a broad population group whose members range from the highest professional and industrial executives to the dime store clerks. Generally, it distinguishes the growing urban and suburban areas from the more rural and farm ones. At the same time, it sets apart the more heterogeneous from the more homogeneous areas. Moreover, the emergent and newer urban and metropolitan areas are more likely to be white collar in composition than the older urban areas.[5] Thus, the concept of the white collar sector is particularly appropriate in an analysis of recent southern urbanization.

Although the white collar variable, as defined by the U.S. Census Bureau, is a pure measure, it is also a composite measure conceptually which embraces elements of urbanism and socio-economic class. The notion of an urban and class basis for the new Republican vote in Dixie is not new. Donald S. Strong has clearly pointed to this phenomenon previously.[6] However, the concept of white collar Republicanism is offered as an advantageous refinement of the notion of urban Republicanism. While the urban and white collar variables are highly but imperfectly correlated, as Table 1 below demonstrates, early analyses in this study indicated that the white collar measure correlated better with recent Republican voting than did the urban one.

TABLE 1

CORRELATIONS BETWEEN PROPORTION WHITE COLLAR AND PROPORTION URBAN, 1960

Deep South		Rim South	
Alabama	.80	Arkansas	.67
Georgia	.65	Florida	.66
Louisiana	.82	North Carolina	.68
Mississippi	.80	Tennessee	.80
South Carolina	.62	Texas	.71
		Virginia	.79

Inasmuch as the U.S. Census Bureau defines urban to be places of 2,500 inhabitants or more,[7] it may be that the urban variable measured across the entire South would represent the effects of many small towns. These would not be the locus for substantial Republican development, which has come to be associated with the rapid metropolitan development of the South. As Havard has observed, "the South made a major leap in its metropolitan development in the decade of the 1950's, during which it moved to the point of having half its population resident in metropolitan areas."[8] Clearly, this demographic change points to the potential for the emergence and persistence of Republican competition. Yet, the a priori selection of certain metropolitan areas for analysis would introduce a subjective bias in the inquiry. It is the great merit of the white collar variable, measured across entire states, that it captures what most people understand by urbanization and metropolitan development without an a priori selection of these areas.

The chapters which follow establish the dominance of the white collar sector as the reliable basis for the new southern Republican vote, with the 1964 and 1972 presidential elections standing apart from the general trend. Further variations on this trend will be observed in the state by state analysis and in the non-presidential vote analysis. The durability of white collar southern Republicanism is important in its own right as evidence of an electoral realignment. Its deeper meaning, however, is still open for probing and analysis. From the perspective of class based electoral cleavages, the new pattern fits well within the context of the national New Deal electoral realignment. Irrespective of the presently ambiguous character of this realignment outside the South, it may be that after a period of insulation and lag, the South is currently repeating the history experienced earlier in the North.

From another perspective, however, white collar southern Republicanism may be considered less an expression of the New Deal alignment and more the political behavior of the sector most likely to depart from the traditional partisanship of the South. This is because this sector contains what Joseph Bensman and Arthur J. Vidich describe as the new middle class, one of whose chief characteristics is opposition to tradition.[9] Clearly, this class has become a likely vehicle for the Republican alternative in southern politics. Thus, what seems to take the form of the New Deal realignment in the South may be the product instead of a very different force than that which sustained class opposition politics in the North.

Levels and Methods of Analysis

Three different measures of change are employed in the following analysis. The simplest measure is the strength of the vote, usually taken at the state level. At this level of inquiry, the southern states have exhibited spectacular change from previous elections, most notably in 1952, 1964, and 1972. However, the percentage distribution at the state level reveals nothing about the forces or cleavages producing the observed change or whether, in fact, these forces differ in one election as opposed to another.

A second and more sophisticated measure is the correlation between votes over time. In the present study the county votes, which ultimately make up the state vote, are correlated over time. The importance of this measure is that it reveals whether the state percentage change of the vote, if any is produced by change in some of the counties or regions below the state level. In the following two chapters correlations between successive presidential election pairs will pinpoint periods of electoral departure and stability through the low and high correlations respectively.

A third level of analysis postulates which cleavages are important in accounting for the vote and introduces controls for them. While a partial correlational analysis could accomplish this, a multiple regression analysis is employed in the present study, for reasons discussed below.

Further rationale for the choice of the correlational and regression techniques merits comment. Linear correlation (r) quantifies the degree of co-variation between two variables. It is useful in the beginning stages of inquiry, when it is important to locate the related variables and to choose for further analysis those which are more rather than less related. The correlation coefficient can cary from (1.0) indicating a perfect positive relationship, through (0.0) indicating no relationship, to (-1.0) indicating a perfect negative relationship. Such a measure is important for making the distinction between the strength of the vote and the quality of the vote. The latter points to the pattern of the distribution of the vote across the units of analysis, the counties, rather than to the size of the overall state party vote. Thus, the county vote proportion contributing to a high state Republican vote in one year and a low Republican vote in another could be highly correlated, assuming that the degree of gain in the former and the fall-off in the latter were distributed equally among all the counties. By contrast, similar strengths of the state Republican vote in different years could be produced by very different types of counties, thus indicating a profound difference in the quality of the vote. Knowledge of both the strength of the vote and the quality of the vote are important for comprehending electoral change. However, knowledge of the quality of the vote, its stability and change, is a theoretically more powerful kind of information.

The principal statistical technique employed in the following analysis is multiple linear regression. While the correlation coefficient (r) represents the closeness of association between two variables, the regression coefficient measures the amount of change in one variable associated with a given change in the other. Multiple regression is an extension of this logic to the instance of more than one independent variable. Thereby, it is possible to measure the amount of change in one variable associated with a given change in the other while simultaneously controlling the effects of the other independent variables.

In the present study, correlational analysis presents an overview of the degree of relationship between elections, thus indicating patterns of stability and departure. Regression analysis then refines the perspective by delineating the dynamics which produce these patterns. This is accomplished by measuring the effects of the three independent variables, the 1940 Republican vote, the 1960 proportion Negro in the population, and the 1960 proportion of the working population in white collar occupations, upon the dependent variable, the later Republican vote. By providing an estimate of the degree of change in the dependent variable, the vote, that occurs on the average for each unit change in the independent variables, the manner in which the independent and dependent variables are related is specified. It is a way of taking typical change in the independent variables and seeing how much change it would make in the dependent variable. By contrast, the correlation coefficient reveals only the degree to which variables may be related, not the manner in which they may be related. For this latter knowledge, the regression equation is essential.

The simple regression equation for the formula of the relationship between one dependent variable and one independent variable is:

$$y = a + bx$$

where

> y is the value of the dependent variable
>
> x is the value of the independent variable
>
> b is the regression coefficient, and
>
> a is the y intercept.

The following analysis pays special attention to the values of (b), the regression coefficient. These values represent a constant which is multiplied by each value of the independent variable, say a county demographic variable in the case of this study, in order to predict the dependent variable score, the vote in this case, for each unit of analysis. The regression coefficient (b) predicts the degree of change in the dependent variable (y) expected for each unit change in the independent variable (x). It is a way of expressing what value the dependent variable (y) would be for a given value of the independent variable (x). If (b) is a positive value, it indicates that one variable rises in value as the other does. The actual numerical value of the coefficient indicates the rate at which they vary together. When (b) equals 1.0 there is a one-to-one relationship between change in the two variables. If (b) is a negative value, it indicates that one value declines as the other rises. From a graphic perspective, the regression coefficient also represents the slope of the line drawn between two points in a scatter diagram, this set of points defined by the values of the variables. While (b) specifies the degree of the slope or the rate of change between the two variables, the y intercept, or the value of (a), indicates the point at which the line crosses the y axis. The y intercept is also the value of the dependent variable when the independent variable equals zero. This is a very interesting coefficient as well, inasmuch as there is a rough correspondence between the overall size of the vote in a state and the values of (a). In years characterized by a great surge in Republican votes, such as 1964 and 1972, the values of (a) are relatively high. Thus, the y intercept alone can also indicate important changes in the vote.

Aside from the specification of how much change in one variable is associated with change in another, there are two further advantages of regression analysis over correlational analysis for the present study. First, while the units of analysis are the counties, the units being compared are the states. These range in size from relatively tiny South Carolina (n=46) to massive Texas (n=254). Regression coefficients are advantageous when the units being compared (the states) are of unequal size - a situation which could yield biased correlations. [10] Secondly, the regression coefficients are not nearly as affected by extreme values of the data, as are the correlation coefficients. [11]

Just as the correlation coefficient reveals aspects of the vote not evident from the overall summary of the vote in a state, so the regression analysis can reveal dynamics of the vote which the summary correlations themselves hide. It is possible that correlational stability can mask considerable variation of the components of the vote which are then revealed by the multiple regression analysis. Thus, this study in comparative voting behavior and electoral cleavages depends upon a successively more precise measurement of electoral cleavages and the forces contributing to them. In this manner, what is common to southern Republicanism throughout the region and what is variable across time and across the states will be evident.

FOOTNOTES

1. William C. Havard, ed., *The Changing Politics of the South* (Baton Rouge: Louisiana State University Press, 1972).

2. See W.S. Robinson, "Ecological Correlations and the Behavior of Individuals," *American Sociological Review*, XV (1950), 351-357. Leo Goodman has rejoined that in some circumstances it is possible to infer individual correlations from ecological correlations. See his "Ecological Regressions and the Behavior of Individuals," *American Sociological Review*, XVIII (December, 1953), 663-664; and, "Some Alternatives to Ecological Correlation," *American Journal of Sociology*, LXIV (May, 1959), 610-625.

3. Samuel Lubell, *The Future of American Politics* (Third ed.: New York: Harper & Row, 1965), pp. 131-155.

4. U.S. Bureau of the Census, *County and City Data Book, 1967* (Washington, D.C.: 1967), p. xxii.

5. On this point see Richard F. Hamilton, *Class and Politics in the United States* (New York: John Wiley & Sons, Inc., 1972), pp. 160, 173.

6. Donald S. Strong, *Urban Republicanism in the South* (University, Alabama: Bureau of Public Administration, 1960). See also his "The Presidential Election in the South, 1952," *Journal of Politics*, XVII (August, 1955), 343-389.

7. *County and City Data Book, 1967*, p. xx.

8. Havard, *The Changing Politics of the South*, p. 13.

9. Joseph Bensman and Arthur J. Vidich, *The New American Society: The Revolution of the Middle Class* (Chicago: Quadrangle Books, 1971), pp. 161-170.

10. H.D. Price, "Micro and Macro Politics: Notes on Research Strategy," in Oliver Garceau, ed., *Political Research and Political Theory* (Cambridge, Mass.: Harvard University Press, 1968), p. 125. See also pp. 102-140, passim, for a sophisticated and sensitive discussion of the uses of individual and aggregate level data.

11. G. David Garson, *Handbook of Political Science Methods* (Boston: Holbrook Press, 1971), p. 191.

Chapter III

Presidential Republicanism: The Deep South

Although the South as a whole has represented the foremost example of sectionalism in American politics, it is the deep South sub-region which has done so most strongly. Here the pre-1952 strength of Republican voting was weaker and the recent resurgence of inter-party competition was more erratic. Here the third-party campaigns in the 1948 and 1968 elections were more warmly received. Dixiecrat pluralities in 1948 as well as all but one of the American Independent party pluralities in 1968, the exception being Arkansas, occurred in the deep South. Similarly, all of Senator Goldwater's 1964 southern presidential pluralities were in the states of the deep South. In all three instances, however, the rim South reactions to these campaigns were warmer and more favorable than those of the non-southern areas. Thus, the states of the southern crescent, stretching from South Carolina to Louisiana, are analogous to an ideal type model of southern politics and may be studied in order to probe and delineate patterns and trends applicable throughout the South.

Electoral Departure and Electoral Stabiility

It is possible to separate analytically two types of southern electoral response of recent years - that which is relatively durable over time and that which is not. That voting change has taken place is obvious - the strength of recent Republican voting indicates as much - but the durability of change is another matter. This question is particularly important for interpreting the meaning of the massive Republican vote in the South in the 1972 presidential election. More generally, the electoral realignment perspective compels attention to the distinction between ephemeral and durable change.

Two types of protest voting have dominated the southern electoral response - one is more economic in character and one is more exclusively white racial protest. It is likely that the more exclusively racially motivated vote would be less stable because neither major party has consistently championed the racist cause. In 1952 many southerners thought that Eisenhower was the candidate of the southern white man, but by 1956 they thought differently. In 1964 the Republicans adopted a "southern strategy" and reaped a rich and unique electoral harvest in the deep South states, but in 1968 southerners who had used the Republican party solely as a vehicle for white racial protest were more comfortable with Wallace than with Nixon. However, in 1972, the choice between President Nixon and Senator George McGovern produced a relatively uniform massive Republican response on the part of the white South. Whether this response indicates the shape of things to come depends upon the future agenda of politics, the stance of Democratic presidential candidates, and the willingness of George Wallace not to lead a third-party campaign. The 1972 response, however, was inconsistent with the more durable trend of recent southern Republican voting. By contrast, the more economically oriented Republican vote is more likely to exhibit stability, not because economic cleavages are themselves intrinsically more stable, but rather because they would be consistent with the on-going New Deal electoral realignment. Of course, this argument assumes the persistence of this national alignment pattern and its continuation in the established mold. Were this alignment era to be replaced by another one, or indeed by an era of no persistent and dominant cleavages, this assumption would not hold. Of these considerations, however, more will be elaborated in the concluding chapter.

The strength of the Republican vote has exhibited wide variability in the states of the deep South in the period following the Second World War. In 1952, 1964, 1968, and 1972 the level of Republican voting here departed sharply from previous levels, as Figure 1 illustrates. Alabama and Mississippi best epitomise this variability. In 1964 they were the most Republican states, while in 1968 they were the least Republican ones, not only in the deep South, but in the nation. In 1972 they were joined by Georgia, Florida, and Oklahoma to become the outstanding Republican states in the nation. The importance of this variability is that it suggests a politics of surge movements which would be antithetical to a stable electoral realignment. Nevertheless, a sharp change in the strength of the vote need not always indicate a sharp shift in its social bases. Thus, it is reasonable to probe correlational patterns and to pay special attention to these junctures. Accordingly, Table 2, below, presents the correlations between successive pairs of presidential elections, and demonstrates that the presidential elections since 1960 have been highly disconnected in their social bases, especially in Alabama, Georgia, and Mississippi. The particular dynamics of these relations are explored in the following state by state analysis.

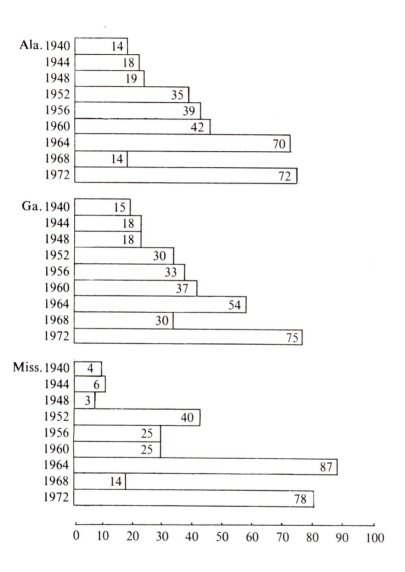

FIGURE 1

Percentage Republican of Total Vote by State, 1940-1972

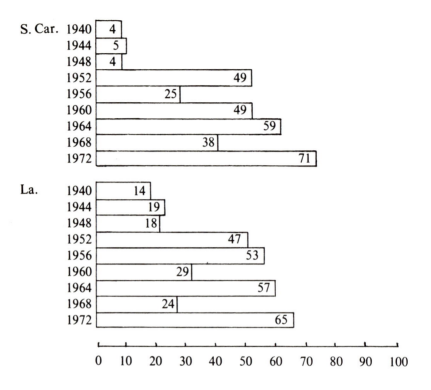

FIGURE 1 - CONTINUED

Sources: Richard M Scammon, ed. *America at the Polls*
                  (Pittsburgh: University of Pittsburgh Press, 1965).

                  Richard M. Scammon, ed., *America Votes 8*
                  (Washington, D.C.: Governmental Affairs Institute, 1970).

                  Congressional Quarterly Weekly Report,. Vol. 31, No. 10,
                  (March 10, 1973).

TABLE 2
CORRELATIONS OF CONTIGUOUS PAIRS OF REPUBLICAN VOTES BY STATE

Pair	Ala.	Ga.	Miss.	S.Car.	La.
1940-44	.97	.72	.82	.62	.27
1944-48	.97	.63	.62	.69	.06
1948-52	.43	.64	.24	-.03	.13
1952-56	.82	.83	.62	.05	.43
1956-60	.90	.80	.59	.33	.05
1960-64	.11	.00	-.16	.82	.65
1964-68	-.38	-.24	-.49	.23	-.14
1968-72	.10	.05	.09	.52	.32

Alabama

During the 1940's Alabama's Republican vote evidenced the greatest stability of any of the deep South states. This stability reflected two conditions. The first is the existence of twelve mountain Republican counties scattered throughout the northern half of the state, of which Winston County is the most famous.[1] The second condition is that these counties were politically isolated from the currents which agitated the Alabama Democrats in 1948. Since Dixiecrat candidate Thurmond was actually the candidate of the Democratic party of Alabama in the state, the schism was confined to the majority party and the Republicans continued to vote in their accustomed ways.

The stability and isolation of Alabama Republicanism was shattered in the 1950's and 1960's as this vote evidenced discontinuities in its strength and correlational patterns. The 1952, 1964, and 1972 surges of electoral strength, together with the evidence of correlational discontinuity from the preceding years indicate that the substantial increment of Republican votes came from counties not strongly Republican in the previous period. In the three-way contest of 1968, the Republican vote fell to its 1940 level for the first time in this entire period. Moreover, the correlation of the 1968 and 1940 votes (.77) was the highest of any of the deep South states and represented a reversal of the departure of 1964. Alabama's unusual

1972 Republican vote was better correlated with the 1964 Republican vote (.32) than with any other presidential vote in Alabama, although the relationship was not an overly strong one. Nevertheless, this relative similarity is important in that it suggests a similar model for both unstable voting patterns. The correlational evidence, therefore, suggests a pattern of electoral departure, subsequent repudiation of the departure, and departure again, casting doubt upon the existence of a general electoral realignment in Alabama.

The determinants of this pattern of departure and "correction" are suggested in the regression coefficients of Table 3. It is apparent that the highly stable quality of the pre-1952 Republican vote was produced almost entirely by the constricted traditionally Republican sector. There is better than a one-to-one relationship between the proportion Republican in 1940 and the proportion Republican in 1944 and 1948. The only other variable which offered a positive contribution to the Alabama Republican vote prior to 1952 was the white collar one in 1948. This is an important finding because it anticipates the strong white collar component of the 1952 Republican vote.

The electoral departure of 1952 was produced by a large contribution to the Republican vote from both the black belt and white collar counties. For the former, this represented a sharp reversal of its previous negative contribution. For the latter, it represented a continuation and strengthening of a trend begun in 1948. The Eisenhower coalition in 1952, therefore, was a broadly based one composed of elements of the traditionally Republican, the rural black belt, and the burgeoning urban and suburban sectors. The Alabama Republican party, at least in terms of its presidential efforts, no longer was isolated from the political currents in the state but was itself a vehicle for these currents.

Alabama's 1952 Republican departure was "corrected" to some extent in 1956. But at the same time the 1952-1956 election pair was also highly correlated and the strength of the Republican vote increased. The stability of the contributions from both the traditionally Republican and white collar sectors account for this tie while the decline in the contribution from the black belt between 1952 and 1956 accounts for the "correction."

The elections of 1952, 1956, and 1960 represent a period of electoral stability in the Alabama Republican vote as reflected both by the strength of the votes and the election pair correlations. Unlike the earlier period,

TABLE 3

REGRESSION COEFFICIENTS FOR REPUBLICAN PRESIDENTIAL VOTES: THE DEEP SOUTH

Election	a	b_{40}	b_n	b_w	R
Alabama County Data (n = 67)					
1944	.06	1.03	-.06	-.05	.98
1948	.00	1.04	-.04	.16	.97
1952	-.08	.97	.44	.53	.80
1956	-.01	1.02	.28	.54	.83
1960	-.01	.93	.30	.66	.83
1964	.76	-.12	.14	-.30	.40
1968	-.05	.50	.00	.37	.84
1972	.94	.00	-.12	-.40	.43
Georgia County Data (n = 159)					
1944	.15	.71	-.13	-.08	.76
1948	.05	.46	-.13	.23	.63
1952	-.09	.39	-.04	.44	.46
1956	.10	.48	-.16	.54	.56
1960	.11	.40	-.09	.58	.50
1964	.42	.05	.32	.10	.42
1968	.12	.24	-.18	.51	.68
1972	.93	-.15	-.23	-.18	.58
Mississippi County Data (N = 82)					
1944	.02	1.29	.00	-.05	.83
1948	.00	.53	.00	.02	.79
1952	-.12	1.78	.45	.94	.78
1956	-.08	2.01	.09	.70	.80
1960	-.01	.75	.13	.57	.62
1964	.82	-1.84	.18	.22	.66
1968	-.02	.38	.03	.42	.65
1972	1.04	-.78	-.52	-.07	.88

TABLE 3 - CONTINUED

Election	a	b_{40}	b_n	b_w	R
South Carolina County Data (n=46)					
1944	.03	.52	-.04	.03	.67
1948	.01	.23	-.05	.12	.67
1952	-.08	.33	.67	1.16	.76
1956	.07	.40	-.15	.72	.65
1960	-.12	-.20	.46	1.58	.67
1964	.20	-.08	.42	.81	.58
1968	.19	-.43	-.15	.87	.70
1972	.92	-.12	-.48	-.10	.87
Louisiana Parish Data (n=64)					
1944	.04	.35	.17	.17	.39
1948	-.12	.88	.04	.38	.81
1952	.22	.12	.22	.44	.31
1956	.32	35	-.10	.51	.48
1960	.04	-.24	.18	.69	.36
1964	.54	-1.02	.51	.14	.52
1968	-.01	.24	-.05	.61	.72
1972	.88	-.27	-.44	.03	.70

Legend:

a	= Y intercept
b_{40}	= Coefficient of proportion Republican, 1940
b_n	= Coefficient of proportion Negro, 1960
b_w	= Coefficient of proportion white collar, 1960
R	= Multiple correlation coefficient

however, when stability was the product of the isolated traditionally Republican counties, the period between 1952 and 1960 was electorally stable due to the sustained similar contribution of the white collar sector as well as the traditionally Republican one. Indeed, the trend was for the white collar contribution to increase steadily from 1948 through 1960.

The 1964 Republican vote represented a severe departure from the previous pattern, both in terms of its strength and its correlation with the 1960 vote. The regression coefficients point to the determinants of this departure. The Goldwater appeal obliterated a fairly stable three-part electoral cleavage which prevailed during the 1952-1960 period. Indeed, in 1964 the contributions of the traditionally Republican and white collar counties became negative and the black belt contribution was diminished sharply, although it remained positive. In interpreting these negative coefficients it is important to remember that the regression coefficient measures the contribution of a particular variable to the vote in comparison with the average vote in the state. In this case, the negative contribution of the white collar sector indicates that this sector's enthusiasm for Goldwater was dwarfed by that of other portions of the Alabama electorate.

Thus, in 1964, class was not a relevant dimension of electoral cleavage here and this is reflected not only by the regression coefficients but by the multiple R, which is quite low. Indeed, race, the issue which held the southern Democrats together for decades, prevailed to the benefit of the Republican vote. Table 4 incorporates with startling success the contribution of the proportion of the electorate which was Negro in 1964 to the Republican vote; it also details the contribution of the three other variables. There was a nearly perfect negative relationship between the size of the Negro electorate and the Republican vote. At the same time, this additional variable explains the diminished contribution of the black belt sector in 1964; controlling Negro voter registration permits the contribution of the black belt sector to exceed 1956 and 1960 levels.

In view of the severe electoral departure of 1964, the three-way contest of 1968 takes on special importance. This election, too, was marked by departure, as the strength of the Republican vote fell to 14 per cent, its level in 1940. This sharp decline in strength raised the issue of whether any of the stabilizing tendencies of the 1952-1960 period remained. The regression coefficients indicate that they did remain. For although the strength of the 1968 vote was similar to that of 1940, its social basis shifted. The contribution from the traditionally Republican sector was down half from the pre-Eisenhower period while that of the white collar sector more than doubled from the 1948 Republican vote. The persistence of this cleavage in Alabama was all the more remarkable given the local appeal of George Wallace in his home state. Thus, although the strength of the Republican vote was very small in 1968, smaller than it was in 1948, it was not the product of the isolated geographically bounded sector but did reflect the re-emergence of the class cleavage which prevailed in the 1950's.

The pattern of the 1972 presidential vote points to another yet not unfamiliar story. The potential for stable cleavages to dominate the character of the vote was eclipsed in this year, in view of the Republican strength throughout the state. The very high value of the y intercept reflects this finding, as it did in 1964 as well. Apparently, relatively stable electoral cleavages were dominant only in the years of Republican development and non-success at the polls. In winning handily, as in 1964 and 1972, the Republican vote assumed the character of a surge movement not confined to traditional and stable boundaries. This is an unstable pattern. While this is what it has taken in the past to produce a Republican victory, it is not a firm basis for predicting future Republican victories. It can not be viewed as a Republican party victory in Alabama.

Georgia

Prior to 1964, Georgia was one of the more stable deep South states, as the correlations between the presidential election pairs indicate. In particular, the 1952 Republican vote did not depart sharply from its 1948 distribution, as in the other deep South states. General stability also characterized Georgia's Republican vote, 1952-1960, as in Alabama. These two states also shared stable voting strength in 1952, 1956, and 1960, in contrast to the pattern in other deep South states. This pattern of relative stability was sharply disrupted in 1964 but was "corrected" somewhat in 1968. However, discontinuity again characterized the vote in the 1972 election.

The regression coefficients suggest the sources of Georgia's relative electoral stability and instability in 1964 and 1972. As in the other states, the contribution from the white collar sector was a prominant and stabilizing factor prior to 1964. Also, the contribution of the 1940 Republican vote was similar between 1948 and 1960. The greatest difference between the Georgia Republican vote and the Republican vote in the other deep South states during this period, however, lies in the behavior of the counties with high proportion of Negroes in their populations. Georgia was the only deep South state in which the black belt did not offer a strong positive contribution to the Republican vote in 1952. This pattern no doubt accounts for Georgia's relative stability during the 1948-1952 juncture. Moreover, the black belt did not abandon its negative contribution until 1964. Thus, the presidential Republican voting coalition in Georgia, prior to 1964, was narrower in scope than in the other states and was based upon the more stable new component, the white collar sector, together with the traditionally Republican sector.

Of all the deep South states, Georgia evidenced the greatest historic loyalty to the Democratic party. Prior to 1964 only Georgia and Arkansas had had a consistent record of loyalty to Democratic presidential nominees, having resisted the temptation to desert the party in response to either the Al Smith nomination in 1928 or the Truman nomination in 1948. The continued stability and lack of Republican inroads in Georgia's black belt between 1952-1960 reflect this historic pattern. A further indication of Georgia's persistent and stable Democratic loyalty is that of all the deep South states, Georgia cast the fewest ballots for third-party or Independent presidential electors in 1956 and 1960.

In 1964 Georgia departed from its recent trend and substituted a racial cleavage for the more stable class one. Republicans scored their highest votes in counties with high Negro populations. Controlling Negro voter registration, as in Table 4, emphasizes the racial cleavage in that year and improves the predictability of the model. But the additional control also permits the reappearance of the class cleavage, even in the racially dominated 1964 election. This is an important finding with implications for the 1968 vote. Georgia's relatively strong Republican vote in 1968, 30 per cent, was based, in part, upon a class cleavage whose persistence can be noticed even in 1964. The same case can not be made for Alabama, where only 14 per cent of the electorate voted Republican in 1968, as the comparable coefficients indicate. This pattern may go far in explaining the different strengths of the Republican vote in these two states in 1968.

This review of electoral patterns in Georgia points to several features which set this state apart from others in the deep South and which augur relatively well for the development of presidential Republicanism. Only Georgia, among the deep South states, had not exhibited, prior to 1972, the extreme surge pattern of Republican voting. Accordingly, in 1952 and 1964, the size of the Republican vote was the smallest of any of the deep South states. It is not surprising that in 1968 only South Carolina Republicanism exceeded Georgia's in terms of actual strength. Party development here may be slower, but may, in the long run, be more firmly established.

Misissippi

Mississippi too evidenced electoral departures parallel to those of Ala-

TABLE 4

REGRESSION COEFFICIENTS BY STATE FOR 1964 REPUBLICAN PRESIDENTIAL VOTE CONTROLLING NEGRO VOTER REGISTRATION*

	a	b_{40}	b_n	b_w	b_r	R
Ala.	.65	-.01	.33	.09	-.91	.60
S. Car.	.22	.15	.48	.83	-.31	.61
Ga.	.41	.03	.47	.25	-.60	.57
La.	.59	-.33	.73	.13	-1.70	.87

Legend:

a = Y intercept

b_{40} = Coefficient of proportion Republican, 1940

b_n = Coefficient of proportion Negro, 1960

b_w = Coefficient of proportion white collar, 1960

b_r = Coefficient of proportion registered Negroes in total registered population

*Note: 1964 voter registration data not available for Mississippi 1962 data used for Georgia

bama and Georgia, but in terms of the extreme character of the response, this state stands apart. Both the 1964 and 1968 Republican presidential votes represented the most extreme departures from their immediate preceding elections. Mississippi best expresses the surge quality of voting which has touched all the deep South states.

A unique condition of Mississippi politics, among the states of the deep South, is that 1940 Republicanism, negligible though it be, was an urban rather than a rural phenomenon. The correlation between the proportion urban in 1960 and the proportion Republican in 1940 is (.47). This likely accounts for the very strong contribution of the traditionally Republican population, measured by b_{40}, in both 1952 and 1956. It thereby reflects the southwide pattern of Republican growth in the urban areas, which are also white collar strongholds, the correlation between the proportion urban in 1960 and the proportion white collar in 1960 being (.80).

Mississippi's miniscule Republican vote, in the years before 1952, was contained within the mold of the 1940 Republican vote, as the regression coefficients of Table 3 indicate. By contrast, in 1952 the surge in the strength of the vote resulted from strong contributions from both the black belt and white collar sectors. The strength of the vote declined in 1956 as the black belt withdrew support for the Republican nominee. Of the three areas of 1952 Eisenhower support, the black belt was the most disenchanted with the Republicans in 1956. Its vote went to an independent slate of electors, whose pattern of support will be noted later. However the white collar sector continued to support Eisenhower in 1956, providing further evidence of its more stable politics. Nevertheless, its contribution declined steadily between 1952 and 1964 — a unique pattern among the states of the South.

As in the other states, the 1964 departure in the Republican voting pattern was not sustained in 1968. Instead, the Mississippi Republican vote then strongly resembled the Alabama one, not only in terms of strength, but in the reassertion of the class cleavage as well. In both states the low level of the vote permitted the emergence of cleavages which were largely obliterated by the landslide of 1964. Despite the precipitous decline in the strength of the vote in 1968, it should not be forgotten that, as in Alabama, while this vote was also low during the 1940's, its basis of support had become much broader in the recent period. The pattern of the vote in 1972 was consistent with that of the other southern states, as the surge Republican vote obliterated pre-existing electoral cleavages. This is not surprising; one would most expect it in Mississippi.

South Carolina

Among the deep South states, Alabama, Georgia, and Mississippi evidenced relative electoral stability in the periods before 1952 and between 1952 and 1960. By contrast, South Carolina and Louisiana were unstable at these times. Among all the states of the South, only South Carolina exhibited virtually no relationship between the electoral patterns of 1948 and 1952 or between those of 1952 and 1956. Yet only South Carolina, among the states of the deep South, exhibited a strong positive relationship between the electoral patterns in 1960 and 1964 and the 1964 and 1968 elections. Furthermore, this state produced Nixon's only deep South plurality in 1968. Equally striking is the correlation (.52) between the 1968 and 1972 Republican presidential votes. These correlations point to a period of electoral stability since 1960 and indicate that the South Carolina electorate has undergone a realignment in recent elections.

At two times prior to 1964 — 1952 and 1960 — presidential Republicanism came very close to capturing a majority of the voters in South Carolina. Undoubtedly, the behavior of Democratic elites played an important role in this pattern. In 1952 South Carolinians could vote for Ike on an Independent elector slate, no doubt solving a problem of conscience for many of them. In 1956 the Independent elector slate supported Senator Harry F. Byrd and captured more votes than the Republican slate, although the Democrats won a plurality. Albert Watson, former U.S. Representative (1963-1971) and Republican candidate for governor in 1970, was prominent in support of the Independent slate in 1956. In addition, Senator J. Strom Thurmond's antipathy to the national Democrats could not have but affected the vitality of the Independent slates during the 1950's. Throughout the early 1960's many state Democrats were switching parties and becoming active in Republican politics. Senator Thurmond switched parties in 1964, in response to the Goldwater campaign, and Representative Watson switched parties in 1965. It is likely that the strength and persistence of recent Republican voting in South Carolina can be attributed in large measure to the conversion of numbers of disaffected Democratic elites.

South Carolina's strong Republican vote in 1952 represented the most dramatic surge in Republican strength of any southern state in that year. This surge from virtually nil Republican strength in 1948 to practically majority Republican strength in 1952 was produced by support from the black belt and white collar sectors which offered the strongest contribution to the Republican vote of any of the deep South states in the latter year. In 1956 the strength of the Republican vote fell by half as the black belt withdrew its support for the Republicans, as was the case in Misissippi. Indeed, in South Carolina it offered a negative contribution that year. Undoubtedly, the exclusion of the strength of the Independent elector slate from the Republican vote was the determining factor in this pattern. In 1960, however, when the Independent elector movement was not a prominent factor in South Carolina, the black belt returned to the Republican fold and, again, the strength of the Republican vote approached majority levels. In 1964 its contribution was similar while in 1968 it withdrew again. Generally, prior to 1972, the strength of South Carolin's Republican vote and the contribution of the black belt have been unstable and have varied together. Here, as elsewhere, the black belt has been an important but unstable source of Republican strength.

The white collar sector's contribution to the Republican vote has been much more stable. Between 1952 and 1968 its effect has been high and positive, although at varying levels. Furthermore, class remained a relevant dimension of electoral cleavage even in 1964, in contrast to the patterns in the other deep South states, where its effect was either negative or modestly positive. Undoubtedly, the high and similar contribution of the white collar sector to the Republican vote in both 1964 and 1968 is what produced the modest correlation between these votes. An electoral realignment is a change in the basis of the vote which persists, which is durable. Prior to 1972, this change was expressed better in South Carolina than in any other deep South state.

Louisiana

The patterns of electoral departure and electoral stability in Louisiana present a special case among the states of the deep South. During the 1940's this was the most markedly unstable state; by contrast, its Republican votes in 1960 and 1964 were correlated nearly as much as those in South Carolina. Moreover, the strength of the Republican vote in Louisiana during the 1940's was relatively high for a deep South state. Thus it is especially important to probe the bases of former and more recent Republicanism here.

Louisiana's 1944 electoral departure resulted from the relatively low contribution of the 1940 Republican vote. At the same time the strength of the Louisiana Republican vote spurted from 14 to 19 per cent and it was the only Republican vote in the deep South supported by the black belt in that year. Even in these early years, the Republican vote was a vehicle for social protest.

Traditional Republicanism in Louisiana is based differently than in any other southern state. Located to the west and south of New Orleans in southern Louisiana are the "sugar bowl" parishes. Their votes represented old Whig tendencies and a concern for the protective tariff on sugar.[2] Louisiana's sharp electoral departure in 1944 occurred as the basis of this vote shifted to include the black belt located in the rural northern Louisiana parishes. The leading Republican parishes in 1944 were in the northern sectors which used Republicanism as an expression of protest against the national Democrats.[3]

In the period prior to 1964, racial cleavage produced a series of varying and unstable contributions to the Republican vote, as it did elsewhere in the deep South. By contrast, the white collar sector's support increased steadily. In 1948 the white collar basis for the Republican vote was anticipated more strongly than in the other southern states and in 1972 this was the only deep South state in which the white collar contribution was not negative.

The 1964 election shattered the pattern of class cleavage and race again became the dominant basis for the vote. The extent of this basis is particularly apparent when Negro voter registration is controlled in Table 4. Furthermore, the inclusion of this additional control improves greatly the predictability of the regression model, the multiple R rising from (.52) to (.87). The 1964 pattern was not a durable one, however, and in 1968 the racial protest vote abandoned the Republican column and the Republican vote was again reduced to its more stable white collar basis.

Louisiana shares with South Carolina a correlational tie between 1960 and 1964 but its basis differs. Louisiana's rural north is Protestant and a traditional stronghold for Longism; south Louisiana is Catholic and hostile to Longism. In most cases Huey Long and his heirs were more popular in rural areas than urban ones. Out of this web of relationships it is possible to weave the connections which tied the 1960 and 1964 electoral patterns which saw higher Republican strength in north Louisiana. In 1960 it was reasonable to expect Protestant north Louisiana to vote Republican because of the influence of religion on the 1960 vote. In 1964 it is plausible to find north Louisiana more responsive to Goldwater's southern strategy as the northern parishes historically have been more intransigent on race than the southern ones. These patterns are reflected in the negative contributions of the traditionally Republican sector, which is in southern Louisiana, to the 1960 and 1964 Republican votes. The analysis of electoral cleavages in Louisisana serves to highlight the different motivational bases which can underpin statistical regularities and aggregate generalizations.

Third-Party Voting

The decline of the solid Democratic South has not always led directly to increased Republican fortunes. More than in any other region in recent years, the South has seen substantial and serious third-party movements. These were prominent in 1948 and 1968 and, to a lesser extent, in 1956 and 1960. The presidential campaign of the American Independent party in 1972 did not represent a serious third-party movement. Indeed, without George Wallace at its head, the American Independent party has become less a "third-party" and more a "minor" party. The difference here reflects the distinction drawn by V.O. Key, Jr. between "recurring, short-lived, minor-party eruptions," and "continuing, doctrinal parties."[4] True third-parties reflect conflicts not contained by one of the major parties in two-party competition. This is an apt description of the Dixiecrat and Independent parties which have played a role in southern politics since 1944, when uninstructed elector slates were on the ballots of Texas and Mississippi. In contrast, there are those minor parties which persist despite the appeals of the major parties and the character of two-party competition. The American Independent party shows signs of following this route.

Third-party strength has been extremely volatile, both across time and across the states, as figure 2 demonstrates. Generally, third-party strength and Republican strength in Dixie have been inversely related. The three presidential elections in which true third-party activity was not manifest - 1952, 1964, and 1972 - witnessed the greatest surge of Republican votes. This suggests that the third-party phenomenon is an important factor in the instability which has characterized some of recent southern Republicanism. The possibility of a realignment, as well as the character of the realignment, turn, in considerable measure, on the third-party phenomenon.

Analyzing the strength and pattern of third-party voting yields insight into the pattern of Republican electoral stability and instability during the

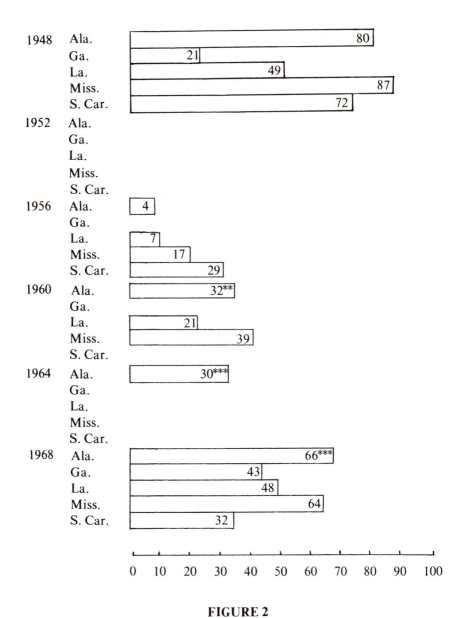

FIGURE 2

Percentage Third Party Votes By State, 1948-1968*

FIGURE 2 - CONTINUED

* Votes representing less than 1.0 per cent of the votes cast are excluded. The figures presented represent almost entirely States' Rights votes. However, in some instances they also include Socialist, Progressive, Prohibition, etc. votes.

** This represents 6/11th of the votes for unpledged Democratic electors since 6 of these 11 electors voted for Byrd instead of Kennedy. It also includes about 4,000 votes for National States' Rights parties and about 4,000 votes for splinter groups.

*** This represents the tally for the Alabama Democratic electors not pledged to the national candidates.

Sources: Richard M. Scammon, ed., *America at the Polls* (Pittsburgh: University of Pittsburgh Press, 1965).

Alexander Heard and Donald S. Strong, *Southern Primaries and Elections* (University: University of Alabama Press, 1950).

Richard M. Scammon, ed. *America Votes 8* (Washington, D.C.: Governmental Affairs Institute, 1970).

1950's. As the correlations in Table 2 indicated, Alabama and Georgia evidenced Republican stability for the election pairs of 1952-1956 and 1956-1960. It was precisely in these two states that third-party slates scored their lowest deep South votes in 1956.

In the case of South Carolina, the absence of third-party voting in 1960 is coupled with both the rise in Republican strength and the start of a durable GOP realignment. During the late 1950's some Democratic elites here began converting to the nascent Republican party, thereby depriving prospective third-party protests a leadership cadre. In the previous election, 1956, the Independent elector slate received wide support in South Carolina, including the black belt, white collar, and miniscule traditional Republican sectors. The white collar support is particularly noteworthy. This pattern of support explains the precipitous decline in white collar support for the Republican slate here in 1956, in contrast to the persistence of similar white collar contributions to the Republican votes in the other deep South states. In view of the past white collar instability in South Carolina, the persistence of its Republican tendency in 1968 is important.

At the other extreme, Louisiana's white collar sector has never contributed positively to third-party movements. Over the years, Dixiecrat and Independent elector slates have appeared before the voters of this state as often or more often than in the other deep South states - notably in 1948, 1956, 1960, and 1968. But, their candidates have drawn strength only from the black belt. By contrast, prior to 1964, the Louisiana white collar sector gave ever increasing support to presidential Republicanism.

In Mississippi the white collar sector has contributed to the third-party vote more consistently than in any other deep South state. No doubt this reflects the broad basis for protest politics in this state. Indeed, in 1956 the white collar sector supported the Independent elector slate in a manner similar to its support for the Dixiecrat one in 1948. Of course in the latter instance, Thurmond carried the standard of the regular Democratic party of Mississippi. This points to the caution one must exercise in using the term "third-party."

The implications of third-party voting for this analysis of southern Republicanism are important prospectively as well as retrospectively. Despite the appeal of the Wallace campaign, the white collar basis of the Republican vote persisted even in 1968.

Below is the Legend for Table 5 (page 51).

a	=	Y intercept
b_{40}	=	Coefficient of proportion Republican, 1940
b_n	=	Coefficient of proportion Negro, 1960
b_w	=	Coefficient of proportion white collar, 1960
R	=	Multiple correlation coefficient

TABLE 5

REGRESSION COEFFICIENTS FOR THIRD
PARTY PRESIDENTIAL ELECTORS

Election	a	b_{40}	b_n	b_w	R
Alabama County Data (n=67)					
1948	1.00	-1.00	.04	-.20	.97
1956	.03	-.02	.14	.11	.71
1968	1.22	-.76	-.68	-.79	.86
Georgia County Data (n=159)					
1948	.04	.15	.41	.15	.44
1968	.81	-.31	-.12	-.74	.47
Mississippi County Data (n=82)					
1948	.69	-1.30	.29	.43	.65
1956	-.13	-.08	.48	.44	.66
1960	.36	-2.10	.27	.15	.56
1968	1.12	-1.56	-.72	-.43	.89
South Carolina County Data (n=46)					
1948	.52	-.23	.68	-.04	.56
1956	-.40	.59	1.03	1.12	.84
1968	.77	-.01	-.37	-1.05	.75
Louisiana Parish Data (n=64)					
1948	.68	-.81	.20	-.30	.46
1956	.05	-.28	.34	-.05	.44
1960	.24	-.82	.43	-.08	.54
1968	.97	-.68	.39	-.69	.67

It has been suggested that third-party voting be viewed as a "half-way house" for an electorate disaffected from its previous partisan home and in the process of shifting to a new home in the other major political party.[5] The potential opportunity for the other major political party is clearly recognized in the notion of a Republican "southern strategy." This strategy was a success in the deep South in 1964. This pattern then did not persist in 1968 because of the Wallace candidacy. From this perspective, therefore, the importance of the Wallace campaign may have been that it held back an impending realignment. Given the character of the 1964 Republican vote, however, this realignment would be quite different from that which prevailed previously. For these reasons, then, the relation between the 1964 and 1972 Republican votes takes on critical importance.

Prior to 1972, the more rural and more traditional sectors of the southern electorate were also the most labile. In voting overwhelmingly Republican for President in 1972, however, the possible contribution of the white collar sector was drowned in a sea of rural votes. This pattern has implications, not only for the realignment of the rural South, but for the character of the statewide Republican vote as well.

The regression coefficients have indicated that the pattern of the 1972 Republican vote was dissimilar to the more stable pattern of Republican voting, but was similar to the 1964 departure pattern. Accordingly, it is instructive to analyze the place of the 1964 Goldwater vote in the subsequent presidential elections. Thus the regression coefficients in Table 6 represent the contribution of three variables to the presidential votes in 1968 and 1972. Instead of controlling the 1940 Republican vote, the 1964 Republican vote is controlled. It has already been observed that the 1964 Republican presidential vote deviated severely from the immediately preceding elections except in the cases of South Carolina and Louisiana. It also deviated severely from the 1968 Republican vote except in the case of South Carolina. The questions remain: What happened to the 1964 Republican vote in 1968? What happened to this vote in 1972?

It is clear that in only one case, South Carolina, was there a positive contribution from the 1964 to the 1968 Republican presidential vote. In the remaining states, the contribution was either nil, as in Louisiana, or negative. The Wallace vote presented just the opposite pattern. The coefficients presented in Tables 3 and 4 emphasized the racial cleavage which dominated the 1964 vote. The continuity between the Goldwater and Wallace votes indicate that this cleavage still existed in 1968, but in a different party. Thus, it further emphasizes why there was such a departure in 1964 and again in 1968. Not surprisingly, the coefficients demonstrate the strongest continuity between the Goldwater and Wallace votes in the state of Mississippi. Also, not surprisingly, in view of the correlational patterns, they point up the unique case of South Carolina and provide additional strong evidence of the electoral realignment in this state, at least prior to 1972.

In 1972 the Goldwater vote was clearly a major component of the Republican vote in all deep South states, in contrast to its fate in four out of five deep south states in 1968. The varying course of this vote in 1968, and 1972 *could* represent a classic expression of an electoral departure which is captured by a third-party protest movement serving as a "halfway house," and is then institutionalized in its new partisan home. This *could* represent a major second - post-white collar - realignment in southern politics.

For more than two decades, therefore, at least since 1948 throughout the entire South, two streams of protest have been winding their way through the region. The racial and economic protest streams have fused together at times and have run separately as well. In a profound sense both reflect the strain and anguish present in a region which is at once undergoing fundamental change very fast and which yet retains a strong regional consciousness. In the decade of the 1960's the rush of these streams continued unabated. The possibility for their durable fusion exists. Whether this will take place depends upon the press of events together with the emerging appeals of both of the major political parties.

TABLE 6
REGRESSION COEFFICIENTS FOR NIXON AND WALLACE
VOTES BY STATE

State	a	b_{64}	b_n	b_w	R
Alabama County Data (n=67)					
Nixon, 1968	.18	-.09	-.17	.19	.64
Wallace, 1968	.57	.54	-.47	-.45	.72
Nixon, 1972	.74	.28	-.18	-.33	.59
Georgia County Data (n=159)					
Nixon, 1968	.18	-.03	-.20	.49	.64
Wallace, 1968	.58	.39	-.19	-.75	.58
Nixon, 1972	.78	.27	-.28	-.20	.73
Mississippi County Data (n=82)					
Nixon, 1968	.22	-.29	.08	.44	.78
Wallace, 1968	.61	.64	-.84	-.69	.94
Nixon, 1972	.83	.25	-.56	-.18	.88
South Carolina County Data (n=46)					
Nixon, 1968	.14	.30	-.28	.52	.76
Wallace, 1968	.79	-.07	-.34	-1.00	.75
Nixon, 1972	.86	.32	-.62	-.39	.93
Louisiana Parish Data (n=64)					
Nixon, 1968	.02	.00	-.06	.62	.72
Wallace, 1968	.76	.30	-.54	-.73	.72
Nixon, 1972	.72	.30	-.59	-.01	.87

Legend:

a	= Y intercept
b_{64}	= Coefficient of proportion Republican, 1940
b_n	= Coefficient of proportion Negro, 1960
b_w	= Coefficient of proportion white collar, 1960
R	= Multiple correlation coefficient

Footnotes

1. This refers to the "Free State of Winston" discussed by Key in *Southern Politics*, p. 282.

2. William C. Havard, *et al.*, *The Louisiana Elections of 1960* (Baton Rouge: Louisiana State University Press, 1963), p. 60.

3. Ecological analysis has been employed more systematically in Louisiana than in any other southern state. See Perry H. Howard, *Political Tendencies in Louisiana* (Revised and Expanded edition, Baton Rouge: Louisiana State University Press, 1971) as well as Howard's chapter in William C. Havard, ed., *The changing Politics of the South* (Baton Rouge: Louisiana State University Press, 1972).

4. V.O. Key, Jr., *Politics, Parties, and Pressure Groups* (Fifth edition, New York: Crowell, 1964), p. 255.

5. Duncan MacRae, Jr. and James A. Meldrum, "Critical Elections in Illinois: 1888-1958," *American Political Science Review*, LIV (September, 1960), 669-683.

Chapter IV

Presidential Republicanism: The Rim South

Greater electoral stability is the chief criterion which distinguishes the politics of the rim South from that of the deep South. Whether expressed in terms of the strength of the Republican presidential vote for better than three decades, the lesser susceptibility to third-party protest movements, or the distribution of the Republican votes in the separate states, the six states surrounding the southern heartland generally stand apart from those of the deep South. Nevertheless, the sub-regional distinction is still viewed as an ideal type whose real manifestations do differ. Thus, while the surge character of the vote, best seen in Mississippi, generally has been absent in the rim South, the states of Florida and Arkansas have exhibited great instability since 1964. It is precisely the advantage of viewing the South through a common perspective that deviations such as these become apparent.

The generally more stable political response of the rim South is a product of demographic factors. Of particular note is the presence of a more extensively distributed traditionally Republican population. This is best expressed in Tennessee, Virginia, North Carolina, and to a lesser extent in Arkansas, where mountain Republicans dominate the traditionally Republican populations. The partisan loyalties of these mountain Republican sectors have their origins in an historic antipathy to the southern cause in the Civil War. These mountain Republican sectors are also overwhelmingly white; historically Republican and Negro concentrations in the population were inversely related. The rim South in general is characterized by fewer Negroes in the population than the deep South.

The greater recent stability of the rim South and the presence of a sizeable traditionally Republican population are related in a positive sense. For the extent of electoral mobilization in a state is limited by the strength and distribution of a traditionally based stable vote. Furthermore, the very presence of a stable minority vote has affected the strategies and options that dominant Democratic elites have felt free to pursue in these states. [1]

The states of the rim South, in sum, can be characterized in terms of the presence of greater traditional Republican populations, fewer Negroes, and less susceptibility to the erratic politics of uninstitutionalized political protest. A major implication of the relatively less prototypically southern response in the rim South is that this sub-region has been more in tune with national currents of opinion than the deep South. The meaning of this implication became abundantly clear in 1964 when presidential Republican strength in the rim South declined from previous levels, reflecting the national trend, at the same time that it reached new heights in the states of the deep South, which ran counter to the national trend. Figure 3 describes graphically the strength of presidential Republicanism in the rim South.

In earlier years as well, the two sub-regions have parted ways. The Republican landslide of 1928 included Republican victories in all the rim South states except Arkansas, but no victories in the deep South. In addition, Dixiecrat pluralities in 1948 were confined exclusively to four of the five deep South states, Georgia being the exception. In 1968 four out of five deep South states cast pluralities for Wallace as compared to only one of the rim South states. Even in 1972, although the strength of the Republican presidential vote was uniformly strong across the entire South, the quality of this vote evidenced some difference between the sub-regions, as the regression coefficients will indicate.

The greater stable quality of the rim South Republican vote is apparent in the correlations between successive presidential election votes in Table 7 below. In sharp contrast to the pattern for the deep South, the 1948-1952 election pair does not indicate discontinuity. Indeed, it was not until the 1960-1964 election juncture that sharp discontinuities in any of these rim South states appeared and at that this occurred in only two states, Arkansas and Florida, and a more modest one appeared in another, Virginia. In three of these six states, however, stability continued to be the norm.

That there are differences between the sub-regions, and indeed, within them, is apparent, but the similarities are at least as important. The differences which do exist between the two sub-regions are ones of degree rather than kind. Thus, the search continues for the bases of the vote, for the existence and stability of electoral cleavages. Again, the Republican vote is explained as a varying product of the contributions of the traditionally Republican, black belt, and white collar sectors. This exploration of southern Republicanism progresses as a theme with variations.

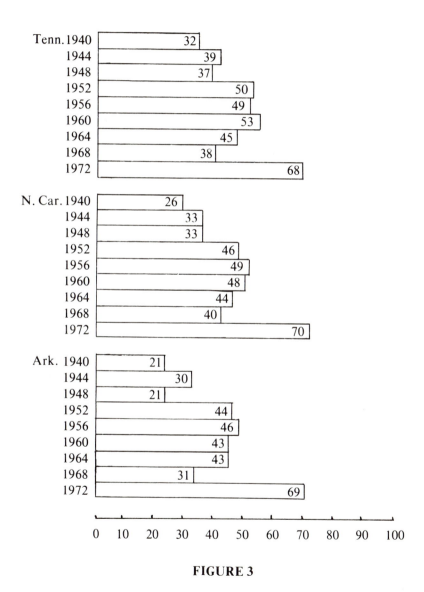

FIGURE 3

Percentage Republican of Total Vote by State, 1940-1972

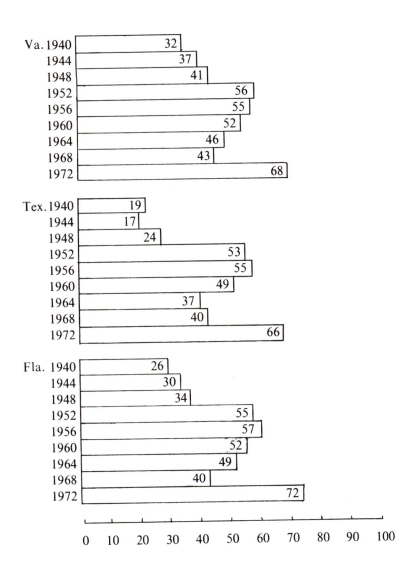

FIGURE 3 - CONTINUED

FIGURE 3 - CONTINUED

Sources: Richard M. Scammon, ed., *America at the Polls* (Pittsburgh: University of Pittsburgh Press, 1965).

Richard M. Scammon, ed., *America Votes 8* (Washington, D.C.: Governmental Affairs Institute, 1970).

Congressional Quarterly Weekly Report, Vol. 31, No. 10, (March 10, 1973).

TABLE 7

CORRELATIONS OF CONTIGUOUS PAIRS OF REPUBLICAN VOTES BY STATE

Pair	Tenn.	N.Car.	Ark.	Va.	Tex.	Fla.
1940-44	.98	.98	.94	.96	.85	.97
1944-48	.96	.97	.90	.93	.80	.94
1948-52	.96	.94	.87	.79	.72	.95
1952-56	.98	.97	.91	.73	.82	.96
1956-60	.96	.97	.80	.80	.72	.93
1960-64	.92	.88	.09	.34	.82	-.04
1964-68	.85	.80	.07	.24	.73	-.18
1968-72	.78	.39	.34	.64	.67	-.25

The Social Bases of the Vote

Tennessee

Of all the southern states, Tennessee has exhibited the greatest electoral stability during the past three decades. This stability is a product of the voting patterns of the traditionally Republican counties in the eastern third of the state. As the coefficients in Table 8 indicate, prior to 1952 this sector offered virtually the only positive contribution to the state's Republican vote. Moreover, it accounted for the Republican presidential vote, virtually alone, as the high values of b_{40} together with the low values of the other variables and the y intercept indicate. Its contribution continued strong in 1964 and 1968 and was not diminished sharply until 1972. In this last year the decline of the traditional Republican sector's contribution occurred as the strength of the vote surged in other regions of the state. This is indicated by the large jump of the value of the y intercept. In this respect, the pattern of the 1972 Republican presidential vote in Tennessee was similar to that of every other southern state. Aside from this shift in the quality of the vote in 1972, Tennessee's traditionally Republican counties constitute a secure resource for the Republican party irrespective of candidates or issues. This traditionally Republican sector alone was never large enough to cast a majority of the state's ballots, but in the three-way contest of 1968 it was an important mainstay of the Republican plurality.

While the contribution of this sector remained consistent, the effects of the other sectors—the white collar and black belt—varied. The surge in Republican voting strength in 1952 was produced by greater Republican voting within these other sectors, as it was in four of the five deep South states. In 1956 both the strength of the Republican vote and the contribution of the white collar sector rose. This relationship is all the more impressive since the black belt contribution declined and the traditionally Republican one remained similar to its 1952 level. However, the contribution of Tennessee's white collar sector in these elections was never as strong nor as dramatic as in the states of the deep South. This suggests that the existence of a sizeable traditional Republican vote is a condition which limits the emergence of a newer cleavage.

Tennessee does not have a large black belt; not very many counties have high proportions of Negroes in the population and only two had populations more than 50 per cent Negro in 1960. Nevertheless, this sector's contribution to the Republican vote has varied in a manner similar to that of the deep South model. The black belt swelled the Republican vote in 1952, abandoned it in 1956, re-entered it in 1960, offered a strong contribution to it in 1964, re-abandoned it in 1968, and was again prominent in 1972.

This review of Tennessee electoral patterns has raised findings which are important in at least two respects. First, the Republican vote has not been nearly as stable as the summary correlations indicated. Secondly, the variation in its electoral patterns has been in the direction taken by the deep South model, especially in regard to the black belt's contribution and the sharp decline in any traditional Republican contribution in 1972.

North Carolina

At first glance North Carolina's Republican vote appears similar to Tennessee's. Both states evidence high stability and both contain sizeable traditionally Republican sectors. But North Carolina's electoral stability results from a different and changing basis, as the regression coefficients in Table 8 indicate.

North Carolina's traditionally Republican sector, unlike the Tennessee one, underwent a secular decline in its contribution to the state's Republican vote. This decline was especially notable in 1952 when the surge of Republican voting strength occurred. In 1956 this sector's contribution held at about its 1952 level but in 1960 and 1964 the decline continued. In 1972 its contribution was even negative, as was common in the deep South. The diminished contribution in 1968 is particularly noteworthy in comparison with the more stable high one of Tennessee's traditionally Republican sector. From the perspective of these coefficients, it is not likely that the contribution of the traditionally Republican sector alone would have been sufficient to effect the Republican plurality in 1968 in North Carolina as might have been the case in Tennessee.

In contrast to every other state in the South, the North Carolina black belt has never contributed positively to the Republican vote. However, its degree of change between 1960 and 1964, in the direction towards a positive contribution, was similar to Tennessee's. In this respect, it reflected a south-wide tendency in 1964 toward Republican support from the black belt. It must be noted, however, that the continued absence of a positive contribution from the coefficient of the proportion Negro in the population reflects the fact that this variable and the proportion Republican in 1940 are collinear.[2]

North Carolina's white collar sector has offered a positive contribution to the Republican vote since 1948. As in other states, the 1948 election marked the beginning of a reorientation of the white collar sector, although it was not until 1952 that its contribution was dramatic. The relative stability of its contribution is indicated by the fact that both in 1964 and 1968 its pattern resembled the 1960 one. Even in 1972, the white collar contribution remained positive, although diminished in value. In that year one finds an identical value for b_w (.14) in both North Carolina and Tennessee at the same time that the mean value for the white collar variable (.26) is identical in both states. This highlights the similarity of the white collar response in both states in 1972.

Despite the particular similarity of the white collar contribution in 1972, there were differences in this and the other independent variables in earlier years. In particular, there is a sharp contrast between the consistency and dominance of the traditional electoral cleavage in Tennessee and the emergence of a class cleavage in North Carolina. Apparently, the emergence of the newer class cleavage is dependent upon the weakening of the traditional one. It also may be that the sharpness of the newer cleavage is dependent upon the absence of the traditional one. Thus, the high level of the white collar coefficients in South Carolina and Mississippi reflected the absence of the strong traditional Republican strength while the more subdued contribution of the white collar sector in Alabama and Georgia reflected the presence of some traditional Republican strength.

A comparison of Tennessee and North Carolina also poses the problem of why there had been a realignment of the traditionally Republican sector in the latter but not the former. A clue to this problem can be found by comparing the strengths and relationships of the mountain Republicans with the Democrats in each of these states. Key observed that the Tennessee mountain Republicans were so strong in the eastern part of the state that the dominant Democrats in the rest of the state granted them hegemony in this region and a reciprocal "live and let live" policy prevailed. The Republicans were permitted to elect two congressmen and local officials in their area in return for not seriously challenging Democratic control of the governorship.[3] By contrast, the North Carolina Democrats did not ignore their mountain areas. They campaigned in these areas and by custom nominated one senator from the west and rotated the governorship

TABLE 8

REGRESSION COEFFICIENTS FOR REPUBLICAN
PRESIDENTIAL VOTES: THE RIM SOUTH

State	a	b_{40}	b_n	b_w	R
Tennessee County Data (n=95)					
1944	.06	1.10	.02	-.12	.98
1948	.01	1.03	-.06	.03	.97
1952	.09	.91	.24	.20	.94
1956	.07	.93	.02	.27	.95
1960	.17	.86	.29	.07	.93
1964	.07	.81	.65	.02	.92
1968	.05	.82	.05	.16	.94
1972	.45	.44	.30	.14	.81
North Carolina County Data (n=100)					
1944	.07	1.01	-.05	.01	.98
1948	.02	.92	-.13	.28	.97
1952	.20	.61	-.25	.45	.89
1956	.21	.62	-.30	.53	.89
1960	.29	.52	-.37	.39	.92
1964	.24	.41	-.06	.31	.78
1968	.24	.45	-.39	.39	.92
1972	.70	-.03	-.16	.13	.38
Arkansas County Data (n=75)					
1944	.03	.95	-.01	.22	.90
1948	-.06	.90	.04	.23	.92
1952	.04	.90	.10	.59	.88
1956	.09	.78	.12	.59	.83
1960	.16	.83	-.04	.32	.84
1964	.23	.33	.24	.28	.48
1968	.07	.65	-.12	.40	.91
1972	.65	.12	-.01	.06	.28

TABLE 8 - CONTINUED

Election	a	b_{40}	b_n	b_w	R
Virginia County and City Data (n = 130)					
1944	.04	1.06	.00	-.01	.96
1948	.04	1.06	-.03	.11	.93
1952	.14	.90	.13	.31	.73
1956	.30	.61	-.06	.23	.63
1960	.33	.46	-.08	.20	.59
1964	.46	.05	.06	-.04	.15
1968	.37	.26	-.32	.16	.80
1972	.79	-.06	-.24	-.08	.49
Texas County Data (n = 254)					
1944	.03	.85	-.15	-.02	.80
1948	-.05	.82	.04	.30	.88
1952	.37	.62	-.25	.17	.66
1956	.28	.61	.08	.37	.61
1960	.28	.33	-.16	.42	.46
1964	.16	.20	.01	.40	.35
1968	.19	.39	-.31	.40	.66
1972	.66	.08	-.13	.09	.22
Florida County Data (n = 67)					
1944	.00	.99	.02	.08	.97
1948	-.12	1.14	.06	.31	.93
1952	-.07	1.16	.34	.58	.90
1956	-.10	1.24	.25	.71	.90
1960	.08	1.02	.14	.36	.84
1964	.61	-.02	-.10	-.16	.17
1968	-.16	.96	.04	.68	.85
1972	1.06	-.09	-.44	-.46	.69

Legend:

a	= Y intercept
b_{40}	= Coefficient of proportion Republican, 1940
b_n	= Coefficient of proportion Negro, 1960
b_w	= Coefficient of proportion white collar, 1960
R	= Multiple correlation coefficient

between western and eastern candidates.[4] Thus, the Tennessee Republicans were considerably more secure than were their counterparts on the other side of the mountains. As a consequence, party loyalties did not become as intense and invariable in North Carolina as in Tennessee.

Arkansas

In both Tennessee and North Carolina, the 1964 election did not constitute a radically different outcome from previous patterns. In Arkansas it did. Here there was virtually no relationship between the 1960 and 1964 votes as well as between the 1964 and 1968 election pairs. Moreover, in 1968, it was in Arkansas that Wallace scored his only rim South electoral plurality. In recent elections therefore, the Arkansas electorate has been both unstable and an unreliable source of Republican votes.

The clue to both the 1964 departure and the 1968 Wallace win lies in the Arkansas traditionally Republican sector which is much smaller than either Tennessee's or North Carolina's. In this respect Arkansas resembles the deep South prototype. Only about one-sixth of Arkansas counties, located to the north and west of Little Rock, offered strong support to the Republicans in 1940. Prior to 1964 and again in 1968 this sector offered strong contributions to the state's Republican vote. In 1964, however, its contribution declined precipitously. At the same time, the strength of the Republican vote remained at 43 per cent, the same as it was in 1960. Thus, the source of these 1964 Republican votes must be sought elsewhere.

The Arkansas black belt replaced the diminished contribution of the traditionally Republican sector in 1964. The contribution of the black belt in that year stands in sharp contrast to both its 1960 negative value and its very modest 1952 value. Undoubtedly, the absence of a strong black belt contribution to the Republican surge in 1952 reflected Arkansas' historic loyalty to the Democratic party, as did Georgia with a similar pattern.

The 1964 pattern implies that a racial cleavage prevailed over a traditional one. Controlling on the proportion of registered Negroes in the electorate, as in Table 9, further supports this interpretation. This control does not affect very much the contributions of the traditionally Republican and white collar sectors, but it does alter sharply the contribution of the black belt. And, altering the model improves its predictability. The susceptibility of the Arkansas electorate to the racist appeal, the relative weakness of the traditionally Republican sector, and the open support for Wallace by many prominent state Democrats—most notably, former governor Orval

Faubus—all explain why Arkansas proved to be Wallace's only rim South win. Furthermore, it appears more than merely coincidental that, in 1948, 1960, and 1968, the third-party efforts fared better in Arkansas than in any other rim South state.

Virginia

Presidential Republicanism is no stranger to Virginia; this commonwealth has voted Republican for President in every election since 1952 with the sole exception of 1964, when it voted Democratic. In this respect, its pattern resembles Tennessee's. In contrast to Tennessee, however, Virginia has been undergoing a broader secular realignment of the basis of the Republican vote. Issues of population movement and enfranchisement are important conditions behind the gradual secular change in alignment patterns in Virginia.

Virginia has witnessed a sizeable increase in the population of certain areas and the level of voting participation has risen considerably. Very likely, the commonwealth would have voted Republican in 1964 were it not for the rapid expansion of the electorate following the adoption of the Twenty-fourth Amendment to the U.S. Constitution which voided the poll tax as a prerequisite to voting in federal elections. This amendment had an immediate impact on Virginia politics inasmuch as the poll tax had been an important device for the maintenance of a small and hence controllable electorate. The dramatic increase in voting participation in 1964 over that of 1960 amounted to 35 per cent.[5] No doubt the lack of a strong correlational tie between the 1960 and 1964 presidential elections reflects this participation explosion.

While a change in law has been one condition behind the expanding Virginia electorate, a second condition is the rapid urban and suuburban development in the counties and cities stretching south and west from the District of Columbia to Richmond and then south and east to the tidewater—the "urban corridor" in Ralph Eisenberg's words.[6] The growth of the population and electorate has been of major consequence for the realignment of Virginia's Democratic party, which is discussed in Chapter VI. This demographic change is also important because it provides a basis for a gradually evolving electorate since 1952. For although both Tennessee and Virginia had a similarly strong traditionally Republican vote prior to 1952, the correlations between successive election pairs point to gradual evolution and discontinuity in Virginia in contrast to the stable patterns of Tennessee.

There is a shift in the pattern of the regression coefficients which reflects the shift in the correlational patterns. In 1952 the contribution from the traditionally Republican sector declined while that of the black belt and white collar sectors increased. In 1956 and 1960, the contribution of b_{40} continued a paced secular decline. In 1964 its decline was precipitous, as it was in Arkansas. Throughout this period the contribution of the black belt reflected that of the deep South model, in terms of its alternating surge and decline dynamic.

What these Virginia trends represent is a blurring and softening of former bases of cleavage.[7] There are two factors which may account for this. One is that the regression model does not present cleavages which are relevant for Virginia. In this regard there is evidence that the dominant cleavage in 1964 was a racial one, as the coefficients in Table 9 indicate. Controlling Negro voter registration augments the contribution from the black belt without seriously disrupting the other coefficients. At the same time, the predictability of the model improves although it is still low.

The second factor which may account for the softening of cleavages is that the distribution of the vote throughout the commonwealth is so similar it can be effectively predicted with low coefficients from independent variables. The crucial factor is effective prediction, as evidenced through a high multiple R. This is, in fact, the case of the 1968 Virginia Republican vote in which the predicting coefficients are not very high but the multiple R is quite high for this state. The existence of a sizeable widely distributed vote is also indicated by the high y intercept.

Texas

Texas is different. It is a state as much western as southern. Its southerness derives principally from its membership in the old Confederacy and its historic loyalty, although not unbroken, to the Democrats. Although in many ways the least "southern" of states, it has not been an easy state for Republicans to win. In 1960 and 1964 it voted Democratic for President, no doubt reflecting the stature of Lyndon Johnson in his home state. But even in 1968 it remained Democratic, alone among the southern states. And in 1972 its substantial Republican majority, 66 per cent, was low in comparison with other southern states.

TABLE 9

REGRESSION COEFFICIENTS FOR 1964 REPUBLICAN PRESIDENTIAL VOTES, CONTROLLING NEGRO VOTER REGISTRATION*

State	a	b_{40}	b_n	b_w	b_r	R
N. Car.	.23	.41	.05	.35	-.22**	.79
Ark.	.21	.35	.68	.32	-.70**	.57
Va.	.46	.04	.37	-.01	-.55	.35
Fla.	.61	-.02	-.09	-.16	.00	.17

Legend:

a　　　= Y intercept

b_{40}　= Coefficient of proportion Republican, 1940

b_n　　= Coefficient of proportion Negro, 1960

b_w　　= Coefficient of proportion white collar, 1960

b_r　　= Coefficient of proportion registered Negroes
　　　　　in total registered population

  * Voter registration data not available for Tennessee and Texas

  ** In North Carolina, 1967 voter registration data employed:
　　 in Arkansas, 1963 voter registration data employed.

There is an ordered pace to the electoral reorientation of the Texas electorate unlike that of any other state. The correlations between successive pairs of presidential elections lack the very high magnitude seen in some states as well as the severe discontinuity present in some elections in some states. This reorientation of the Texas electorate involves the movement of the Republican base from its traditional source of strength to its new constituency in the white collar sector.

Beginning in 1948, the Republican vote received support from the white collar sector, and even in 1964 this sector continued to support the Republican vote in about the same manner as it did in 1956 and 1960. At the same time the size of the Republican vote declined. Thus, during this period the white collar sector remained a consistent "core" of Republican strength. This pattern continued in a similar fashion in 1968, again illustrating the stable class cleavage in Texas politics. Even in 1972 the white collar contribution remained positive although diminished in strength. This is not surprising for what may be the "least southern" of southern states. Furthermore, there is a tradition in Texas for the opposition of economic conservatives and economic liberals in Democratic party factionalism.[8] Since 1948, the economic conservatives have felt quite comfortable with presidential Republicanism.

While the contribution of the white collar sector has been generally stable, that of the traditionally Republican sector has been declining. It is important to note that the 1940 Republican vote in Texas, the measure of traditional Republicanism, is not of the southern Appalachian variety, but rather is composed of descendants of nineteenth century immigrant residents in the "German counties" in the plateau regions to the north and west of Austin,[9] and is also found in the panhandle counties where the partisan roots of the inhabitants owe much to their midwestern origins.

The weakening of this traditionally Republican vote in both relative and absolute terms has occurred in two ways in Texas. Soukup, McCleskey, and Holloway point out that the German counties can no longer be distinguished in their voting records from other counties.[10] The state-wide distribution of the Republican vote has broadened. Moreover, it is evident in data they present that in most of these counties, the 1956 Republican vote exceeded the 1952 levels, but in 1960 the Republican percentage declined below 1952 levels.[11] The reason for this decline lies in the Democratic proclivity of the burgeoning Mexican-American electorate. Controlling the vote of this group would reveal higher contributions from the traditionally Republican sector, especially in 1960. The presence of the Mexican-American population is a major feature which differentiates Texas from the southern states. The U.S. Census Bureau's report of the proportion foreign stock, found in the *City and County Data Book,* is a convenient indicator of the distribution of Mexican-Americans in Texas.[12] As a minority group, they are a counterpart to the Negro population in the other southern states. Accordingly, early data analyses for this study included the proportion foreign stock in the regression equation. While this additional variable had no effect on the white collar variable, it did make a substantial difference for the contribution of the traditionally Republican sector.

Florida

Florida represents a unique case among the states of the rim South. Prior to 1964, its electoral patterns were as stable as the most stable rim South states. Yet the electoral discontinuity of Florida's 1960-1964 Republican vote approached that of Mississippi, the most unstable deep South state at this juncture. Electoral discontinuity, evidenced by negative correlations, continued to characterize Florida's Republican vote in the 1964-1968 election pair as well as in the 1968-1972 one. No other state, throughout the entire South, evidenced such discontinuity for these three successive election pairs.

Aside from the extreme discontinuity in recent years, the pattern of the social basis of the Republican vote was similar to that of the other southern states. The rising Republican strength in the Sunshine State was the product of a broadening of the social basis for the vote. The 1940 Republican vote alone accounted for almost all of the 1944 vote. In 1948 the basis for the vote expanded to include the white collar sector. The 1952 surge in Republican strength was produced by the swing of the black belt, in addition to the support of the other two sectors. In that year, the contribution of the white collar sector was substantial and in 1956 it was even greater. In 1960 and 1964, however, it evidenced a secular decline while in 1968 it again offered a strong contribution. The white collar contribution in 1972 was negative, as it was in most deep South states. Again, the character of electoral cleavages in Florida in recent years is more akin to the deep South than to the rim South model.

The behavior of Florida's traditionally Republican sector constitutes a singular variation in this tale of southern politics. In most of the states, its contribution declined throughout the period under study. By contrast, in Florida it exhibited an increase in support from 1944 through 1956 and even in 1960 its contribution remained very high. The composition of this sector and the course of Florida politics account for this anomaly. Republican strength in 1940 was located in south Florida, which was populated by new migrants who were disproportionately old and retired or young and ambitious. In terms of the simple thesis of class interest this group's Republicanism is plausible. More than the case of class interest politics, however, the newness of their Florida residence sets this group apart from long-settled traditionally Democratic Florida society. Throughout the South, Republican politics served as a social outlet for new residents who were not completely comfortable in their new communities.[13] Quite simply, areas which were Republican in the 1940's continued to attract migrants — hence, the increasing contribution of Florida's traditionally Republican sector. And this sector's contribution was an important factor in the stability of Florida's Republican vote prior to 1964.

The 1964 presidential election is a watershed in Florida politics in that it demarcates the earlier stable period from the later unstable one. Unfortunately, the major regression model in this study is not at all efficacious for predicting this vote. Quite possibly, this is due to the regional split in Florida politics which was crucially important in that year. Panhandle Florida is part of the old deep South; peninsular Florida, especially the southern half of the peninsula, is the scene of the vast migration which this state attracts. Prior to 1964 the Republican vote was disproportionately concentrated in the southern part of the state; in 1964 as well as 1972 it was disproportionately concentrated in the less populous rural counties of northern Florida. Table 10, below, attests dramatically to this split. In correlating the strength of the Republican vote with the size of the population it is clear that in all presidential election years except 1964 and 1972, the two were positively related; in 1964 and 1972 they were negatively related.

Third-Party Voting

The states of the rim South have witnessed some third-party activity, but its occurrence has not been as often nor nearly as strong as in the states of the deep South. Prior to the 1968 election, the Dixiecrat movement in 1948 constituted the only serious third-party effort. Indeed, for this earlier period, North Carolina did not experience any third-party activity at all

TABLE 10

CORRELATIONS OF PROPORTION REPUBLICAN
PRESIDENTIAL VOTE
WITH POPULATION (1960) BY COUNTIES:
FLORIDA

Election	Correlation
1940	.36
1944	.38
1948	.40
1952	.38
1956	.35
1960	.24
1964	-.34
1968	.33
1972	-.47

except for the 1948 instance, and Florida cast only a handful of third-party ballots in 1952 and 1956. In the deep South third-party voting was much greater in 1956 and 1960 than in the rim South. Figure 4 presents the distribution of these ballots by state and by year throughout the rim South. Excluding 1948 and 1968 these votes are too few to notice seriously.

Not only has third-party voting been considerably less pronounced in the states of the rim South, but its basis of support has been much narrower. Indeed, in no instance in the rim South did it receive a strong positive contribution from the white collar sector, as Table 11 indicates. By

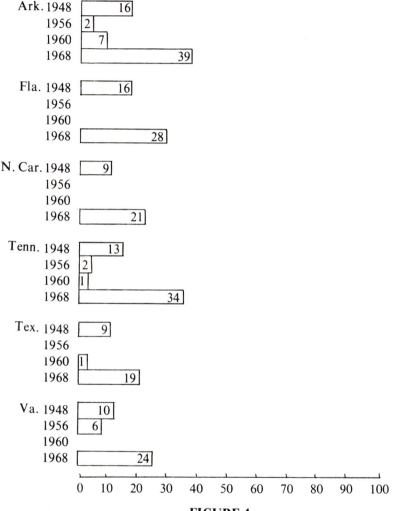

FIGURE 4
Percentage Third Party Votes by State, 1948-1968

Sources: Richard M. Scammon, ed., *America to the Polls*
(Pittsburgh: University of Pittsburgh Press, 1965).

Alexander Heard and Donald S. Strong, *Southern Primaries
and Elections* (University: University of Alabama Press, 1950).

Richard M. Scammon, ed., *America Votes 8* (Washington,
D.C.: Governmental Affairs Institute, 1970).

TABLE 11

REGRESSION COEFFICIENTS FOR THIRD PARTY
PRESIDENTIAL ELECTORS: THE RIM SOUTH

Election	a	b_{40}	b_n	b_w	R
Tennessee County Data (n=95)					
1948	.08	-.12	.79	-.06	.90
1956	.00	.05	.36	-.14	.73
1968	.61	-.56	.05	-.22	.82
Arkansas County Data (n=75)					
1948	.05	-.05	.62	.03	.85
1960	.07	-.15	.07	.02	.70
1968	.72	-.72	-.09	-.52	.76
Virginia County and City Data (n=130)					
1948	.08	.00	.24	-.08	.55
1956	.00	.02	.29	-.01	.62
1968	.44	-.34	.08	-.34	.69
Texas County Data (n=254)					
1944*	.04	.12	.16	.08	.38
1948	.03	-.01	.48	.01	.75
1968	.28	-.24	.34	-.16	.57
Florida County Data (n=67)					
1948	.12	-.11	.48	.01	.63
1968	1.22	-1.15	-.49	-1.16	.84

North Carolina County Data (n = 100)

1948	.09	-.12	-.05	.10	.29
1968	.49	-.42	.21	-.41	.84

* Texas Regulars

Legend:

a = Y intercept

b_{40} = Coefficient of proportion Republican 1940

b_n = Coefficient of proportion Negro, 1960

b_w = Coefficient of proportion white collar, 1960

R = Multiple correlation coefficient

contrast, in almost every instance, the third-party vote received strong positive support from the black belt. In this latter respect, these states share a common feature with the states of the deep South.

As in the states of the deep South, the 1968 and 1972 elections provide an opportunity to examine the effects of the 1964 Goldwater vote upon later Nixon and Wallace votes. This comparison is more crucial in the case of the deep South where electoral departure was the dominant pattern in 1964. In the rim South states, electoral stability was as prominent as electoral departure in 1964. Because electoral departure did characterize Arkansas, Virginia, and Florida, this is an important comparison. (Table 12)

This line of inquiry reveals something of the basis for Florida's recent instability. In this state, the 1964 Goldwater vote, which was sharply different from previous Republican votes, moved into the Wallace column in 1968 in a decisive manner. Yet this Goldwater vote was a component of Nixon's 1972 vote. Thus, electoral patterns in Florida strongly resembled those of the deep South. In contrast to the Florida pattern, the Arkansas

TABLE 12

REGRESSION COEFFICIENTS FOR NIXON AND WALLACE VOTES BY STATE: THE RIM SOUTH

State	a	b_{64}	b_n	b_w	R
Tennessee County Data (n=95)					
Nixon, 1968	.00	.96	-.62	.13	.96
Wallace, 1968	.63	-.63	.51	-.20	.82
Nixon, 1972	.41	.56	-.06	.13	.89
North Carolina County Data (n=100)					
Nixon, 1968	.24	.58	-.54	.05	.94
Wallace, 1968	.24	.01	.52	-.16	.78
Nixon, 1972	.46	.43	.02	.12	.59
Arkansas County Data (n=75)					
Nixon, 1968	.16	.42	-.46	.14	.81
Wallace, 1968	.45	-.02	.24	-.28	.50
Nixon, 1972	.53	.46	-.11	-.05	.62
Virginia County and City Data (n=130)					
Nixon, 1968	.31	.40	-.45	.07	.83
Wallace, 1968	.15	.24	.20	-.17	.59
Nixon, 1972	.48	.55	-.23	-.01	.79
Texas County Data (n=254)					
Nixon, 1968	.13	.72	-.36	.08	.83
Wallace, 1968	.16	.32	.42	-.29	.64
Nixon, 1972	.54	.69	-.13	-.18	.74

Florida County Data (n=67)

Nixon, 1968	.08	-.28	-.12	1.10	.62
Wallace, 1968	.62	.86	-.25	-1.58	.69
Nixon, 1972	.79	.43	-.39	-.43	.82

Legend:

a   = Y intercept

b_{64} = Coefficient of proportion Republicans, 1964

b_n = Coefficient of proportion Negro, 1960

b_w = Coefficient of proportion white collar, 1960

R   = Multiple correlation coefficient

1964 Republican vote stayed with the Republicans in 1968 *and* 1972. In Virginia, a similar pattern prevailed. However, it should be noted that in both Virginia and Texas, the 1964 Republican vote contributed to both the Nixon and the Wallace votes in 1968. This pattern stands in contrast to that of the deep South states, where the Goldwater vote moved clearly into either the Nixon or Wallace columns, but not both.

In comprehending this puzzling persistence of the Goldwater vote in both the Nixon and Wallace votes in 1968, it is important to note that the split pattern is most prominent in Virginia and Texas—the two states in which the distribution of the 1964 Republican vote was part of a gradual reorientation which had been evident in the elections prior to that year. Where the 1964 Republican vote was not a departure at all, as in Tennessee, or where it was an abrupt departure, as in Arkansas or Florida, this dual movement of the Goldwater vote did not occur. To some extent, therefore, where there has been a gradual reorientation of the electorate there has also been an extension of inter-party competition throughout the state and a blurring of formerly sharper lines of cleavage. The ability of both Nixon and Wallace to draw support from a common basis, as in Virginia and Texas in 1968, reflects this secular change.

Conclusions

Two dominant conclusions emerge from this review of southern Republican voting patterns across the South, especially in view of the patterns of the past three presidential elections. First, there has been a realignment of the southern electorate which was clearly apparent in the 1968 voting pattern. The white collar sector was once again the dominant new basis for the Republican vote. The three-way contest of that year was, in one sense, the acid test of southern Republicanism because it compelled the party to fall back upon the support of its most reliable partisans, the one who would constitute the essential core of votes for a durable realignment. This also points to the likely basis for the development of party organizational cadres and structures. Unquestionably, there was a broader basis for Republican voting in 1968 than in 1940.

There was a general difference of emphasis between the cleavages in the two sub-regions in 1968 which merits notice. In the deep South, with but one exception — Alabama — the white collar sector offered a stronger contribution to the Republican vote than did the traditionally Republican one, which was still a factor in Alabama. In the rim South states, with the exception of Texas, the opposite pattern prevailed. In this sub-region there was a greater contribution from the traditionally Republican sector than the white collar one.

The year 1968 was a most unusual year in twentieth century southern politics. For in this year the southern voter could chose among three distinct candidacies and each one represented a highly serious effort with a credible chance of victory, especially in the South. Admittedly, this chance of victory refers more to the condition of the Republicans and American Independents in Dixie than the Democrats in that year. Nevertheless, the unusual feature of this kind of competition is that it yielded an unusually clear segmentation of the southern electorate. Such a clear demarcation of electoral tendencies, however, is not the usual result in two-party, majority seeking, relatively evenly balanced, inter-party competition. To be sure, the year 1972 was also unusual, as the model of evenly balanced competition ill fits the reality of the Nixon-McGovern contest.

Unusual years are a source of difficulty in gauging future political patterns. Nevertheless, there is one feature of the 1972 result in the South which is not unusual. Prior to 1972, the 1964 Republican vote was a unique event. It is no longer so and its quality was apparent again in 1972. The three-way contest of 1968 held apart electoral forces which President

Nixon succeeded in uniting in 1972. These forces were present in the Goldwater vote of 1964. It has been commonly observed that President Nixon's landslide, especially in the South, was produced by the combination of the 1968 Nixon and Wallace votes. The regression coefficients presented earlier provide additional insight into this phenomenon. In particular they pinpoint the relationship of both the 1972 and 1968 votes to the 1964 Republican vote. Table 8 demonstrated the similar quality of the Republican votes in 1972 and 1964 while Table 12 demonstrated the prominence of the 1964 Republican vote in the 1972 one. These patterns suggest the possibility of a second major realignment, a post-white collar-based stage of southern Republcanism. There is enough in these three past presidential elections to suggest that 1964 and 1972 represent a possible new routine pattern and that Republican votes in 1968 represented the expression of an earlier voting pattern.

Two decades experience with presidential Republicanism has revealed two different models for the aggregate voting pattern — the white collar and post-white collar patterns. The white collar realignment has been the more stable of the two and is likely to appear again whenever Republican voting strength is in the minority or evenly competitive with Democratic strength. Throughout this period, the vote of the rural South has been a fluid commodity in presidential politics and there is no reason why its fluidity could not continue in the future, depending upon the choices presented to it and the concerns of the times. What would be new in this situation would be not the demise of one electoral alignment and its replacement by another, but the persistence of two patterns which fluctuate between themselves in some manner over time.

FOOTNOTES

1. Key demonstrated that the prominence of the Republican minorities in the various states was an important condition affecting the response of Democratic elites to the Dixiecrats of 1948. See his *Southern Politics*, pp. 336 ff.

2. This refers to the problem of multicollinearity, in which two independent variables are highly related. Consequently, the effect of one of the variables may be subdued in a multiple regression equation. Of all the states in the South, North Carolina poses the problem of multicollinearity most strongly. The correlation between the proportion Republican in 1940 and the proportion Negro in 1960 is (-.78).

3. Key, *Southern Politics*, p. 79.

4. *Ibid.*, p. 219.

5. Ralph Eisenberg, "Virginia: The Emergence of Two-Party Politics," in William C. Havard, (ed.), *The Changing Politics of the South* (Baton Rouge: Louisiana State University Press, 1972), p. 58.

6. *Ibid.*, p. 60 ff.

7. One complicating factor in the analysis of Virginia is that the units of analysis are both counties and independent cities and that the number of the latter have grown considerably since 1940. Only the independent cities in existence by 1967 are used in the analysis.

8. See O. Douglas Weeks, "Texas: Land of Conservative Expansiveness," in William C. Havard, (ed.), *The Changing Politics of the South* (Baton Rouge: Louisiana State University Press, 1972) and James R. Soukup, Clifton McCleskey and Harry Holloway, *Party and Factional Division in Texas* (Austin: University of Texas Press, 1964).

9. Soukup, McCleskey and Holloway, *and Factional Division in Texas*, pp. 36-40.

10. *Ibid.* p. 39.

11. *Ibid.* p. 38.

12. This variable comprises "both the foreign-born population and the native population of foreign or mixed parentage." U.S. Bureau of the Census, *County and City Data Book, 1967* (Washington, D.C.: Government Printing Office,1967), p. xx. In 1960, 27 out of Texas' 254 counties contained populations which were at least 20 per cent foreign stock.

13. This phenomenon has also been noted by Kenneth N. Vines, See his *Two Parties for Shreveport* (Case Sudies in Eagleton Foundation Series, New York: Holt, 1959).

Chapter V

The Diffusion of Competition: The Deep South

The most important criterion for the electoral change which is realignment is the durability or persistence of the new pattern—in a word its institutionalization. Past electoral realignments have also touched, in time, voting beneath the presidential level. Thus, the continuity and stability of new presidential electoral cleavages, and their diffusion to other levels of competition, are important aspects of electoral realignment.

The 1960's witnessed the emergence of serious and sometimes successful Republican competition on the non-presidential level. In the 1950's, southern Republicanism was largely a presidential phenomenon; by the early and mid 1960's, it had become much broader in scope. This represents an important development. Previously, Republican voting, especially in the deep South, was akin to a dalliance. In no sense did it constitute a serious challenge to Democratic dominance at the state level. Republicans then were less interested in winning elections than in winning patronage and attending the party's national conventions.

So different had southern politics become by 1972, that this was the only region in the country in which Republicans did well in both presidential and non-presidential voting. In that year state Republican parties in each of the five deep South states met the challenge of competition and vigorously contested for U.S. Senate seats.

The analysis of non-presidential Republicanism proceeds on two levels. The first concerns the social bases of the vote. Here, the general persistence of the pattern of Republican voting dominant on the presidential level in 1952 through 1960 and again in 1968 amply demonstrates the exceptional quality of the 1964 and 1972 Republican votes. This suggests three possible interpretations of present and future politics. The first is that the patterns of voting in 1964 and 1972 are not likely to be durable and are not reliable indicators of Republican development, which would be more appropriately observed on the non-presidential level. The second possibility is that presidential and non-presidential elections are becoming increasingly separate phenomena. The national outcome of the 1972 elections—a Republican victory on the presidential level and a Democratic one outside the presidential level—illustrates this outcome. A third possibility is that if the 1964 and 1972 voting patterns in the South represent the dominant character of future southern presidential politics, it may be only a matter of time until the non-presidential vote aligns with this pattern as well. Irrespective of whichever of these interpretations stands the test of time, the diffusion of competition to the non-presidential level is a very important step in its own right and became possible only because of the experience of the voting breakthrough on the presidential level.

The second dimension of this analysis focuses on the strategies and appeals employed by the different candidates. Thus, in one sense, this is an analysis of the effects of presidental Republicanism for non-presidential competition. In a related sense it is a study of the uses made of presidential competition by those competing for the offices of United States senator and governor. While the congressional vote would also be a very important index to the diffusion of inter-party competition, it would represent an additional level of diffusion and is beyond the scope of the present study.

The Goldwater Impact on the Deep South

The major questions regarding non-presidential competition in the states of the deep South turn upon the effects of Senator Barry Goldwater's presidential candidacy. For here non-presidential Republican competition emerged full-blown more suddenly than in the rim South states. The very slating of Republican candidates for U.S. senator and governor, not to speak of their campaigning seriously, was virtually unknown in this sub-region prior to the 1960's. By contrast, in the states of the rim South there had been a tradition of slating candidates for these offices on occasion, even if the outcome in the general election was a foregone conclusion.

The importance of Goldwater's candidacy can be posed from two separate perspectives. The first concerns its meaning to deep South Republicans in the years prior and up to the general election of 1964. The years of the early 1960's witnessed an increasingly liberal, especially on matters of race, national Democratic administration which was anathema to the traditional outlook of the white South. The altered status of the South in its ancestral party was more tolerable in the previous decade when the national administration was not a Democratic one. For many southern conservatives, the appeal of Senator Goldwater and his prospective candidacy for the presidency was an exceedingly welcome alternative as the 1964 election approached and was a stimulus to Republican party organizational development. Furthermore, it provided a unique opportunity for ambitious men to use the Republican party vehicle and its emerging appeal in order to challenge veteran Democratic office holders who had never known serious competition in the general election.

Three elections in particular pointed to the new electoral opportunities in the South—the 1962 U.S. senatorial campaigns in Alabama, South Carolina, and Louisiana. In Alabama James Martin came within 6,000 votes of ousting Senator Lister Hill; in South Carolina William D. Workman received 45 per cent of the vote against Senator Olin D. Johnston; and in Louisiana, Taylor W. O'Hearn polled 24 per cent of the vote against Senator Russell Long. In each case the Republican effort benefited from tying these Democrats to the increasingly unpopular Kennedy administration. The surprisingly large tally of Republican votes encouraged Goldwater's southern strategists. And together with the Senator's deep South landslide in the 1964 presidential election, the 1962 results greatly encouraged the Republicans to mount serious challenges in the 1966 off-year elections. From the perspective of hindsight, these 1966 expectations were ill-founded.

From another major perspective the relationship between the Republican presidential effort in 1964 and the subsequent statewide contests, especially those of 1966, is of crucial importance. As demonstrated previously, the 1964 election pattern registered a sharp departure from previous patterns in four of the five deep South states. In these states, Goldwater interrupted a trend which was first strongly apparent in 1952. The 1966 elections were the first test of whether this 1964 outcome was a temporary departure from more established patterns or whether it was itself the critical election which heralded a new realignment. With the passage of time, this use of the 1966 voting patterns is less important. Nevertheless, the transferability of presidential voting patterns to non-presidential levels is of theoretical importance to an inquiry into electoral realignment. New presidential voting patterns should be confirmed utlimately, if there be a realignment, by their approximate replication beneath the presidential level.

In 1966 only one deep South Republican, South Carolina Senator Strom Thurmond, received a landslide vote—62 per cent compared to Goldwater's 59 per cent in that state. And, while other Republican candidates in South Carolina and Georgia ran well, though not winning, candidates in Alabama and Mississippi ran poorly. This outcome suggests that the Goldwater breakthrough in 1964 did not automatically result in Republican

TABLE 13

CORRELATIONS OF REPUBLICAN PRESIDENTIAL VOTES, 1960-1972, WITH REPUBLICAN SENATORIAL AND GUBERNATORIAL VOTES, 1962-1972

State	Contest	r, 1960	r, 1964	r, 1968	r, 1972
Alabama					
1962 Senatorial	(Martin v. Hill)	.31	.82	-.18	.16
1966 Gubernatorial	(Martin v. Wallace)	.52	-.38	.75	-.03
1966 Senatorial	(Grenier v. Sparkman)	.65	.16	.59	.34
1968 Senatorial	(Hooper v. Allen)	.52	-.06	.74	.08
1972 Senatorial	(Blount v. Sparkman)	.58	.21	.59	.44
Georgia					
1966 Gubernatorial	(Callaway v. Maddox)	.48	.18	.50	-.25
1968 Senatorial	(Patton v. Talmadge)	.55	.16	.66	.00
1970 Gubernatorial	(Suitt v. Carter)	.51	-.21	.84	-.01
1972 Senatorial	(Thompson v. Nunn)	.39	.22	.39	.26

Mississippi				
1963 Gubernatorial	(Phillips v. Johnson)	.63	-.36	.68	.03
1966 Senatorial	(Walker v. Eastland)	-.17	.22	-.16	-.05
1967 Gubernatorial	(Phillips v. Williams)	.45	-.08	.42	-.54
1972 Senatorial	(Carmichael v. Eastland)	.05	.18	-.03	.05
South Carolina				
1962 Senatorial	(Workman v. Johnston)	.93	.83	.43	-.15
1966 Gubernatorial	(Rogers v. McNair)	.61	.58	.44	.16
1966 Senatorial	(Parker v. Hollings)	.41	.36	.55	.53
1966 Senatorial	(Thurmond v. Morrah)	.43	.43	.69	.62
1968 Senatorial	(Parker v. Hollings)	.22	.20	.66	.71
1970 Gubernatorial	(Watson v. West)	.58	.54	.50	.34
1972 Senatorial	(Thurmond v. Zeigler)	-.02	.06	.55	.91
Louisiana				
1962 Senatorial	(O'Hearn v. Long)	.79	.81	.15	.11
1964 Gubernatorial	(Lyons v. McKeithan)	.44	.18	.60	-.10
1972 Gubernatorial	(Treen v. Edwards)	.78	.74	.13	.49
1972 Senatorial	(Toledano v. Johnston, McKeithen)	.01	-.23	.68	.37

strength in 1966. Further evidence of the discontinuity between the 1964 and 1966 votes is found among the correlation coefficients of Table 13. While the Republican votes in the three prominent senate races of 1962, mentioned previously, were highly correlated with the Goldwater vote, the later senatorial and gubernatorial votes were not. This outcome repudiates the basic rationale of the Goldwater candidacy, from the perspective of southern Republican leaders, who had seen in Goldwater the champion who would finally break the hold of the Democrats on the southern electorate to the benefit of other Republican candidates who would follow. Apparently, the cracking of the solidly Democratic South below the presidential level was not as easy as had been presumed.

To date, only one deep South Republican has actually been elected in these contests for U.S. senator and governor. He is South Carolina's Strom Thurmond who has twice been elected as a Republican and by landslide proportions. Moreover, South Carolina is the only one of these deep South states which has been characterized both by Republican strength in these state-wide contests and continuity between these votes and recent Republican presidential ones. Again, this highlights the durable realignment in South Carolina politics. The following state by state analysis will probe the more variable and more limited Republican response in these different states.

Alabama

First and last, Republican fortunes at the state level here center around the person and political position of George C. Wallace, who has dominated the state since 1962. Quite simply, when Wallace has permitted it, Republicans have run well at the polls; otherwise, they have not. And Alabama's Republican party, although invigorated in the 1960's, has failed to win a statewide contest in either event.

Once, before these facts became clear, there was considerable hope for Alabama Republicanism. James Martin, a Gadsden businessman, polled a near majority in the 1962 U.S. Senatorial election and encouraged speculation that a durable electoral realignment might be imminent.[1] The pattern of Martin's vote clearly anticipated the Goldwater pattern of two years later, as the correlations in Table 13 indicated. Nevertheless, this change was short-lived. For when Martin, who was elected to Congress in the Goldwater sweep of 1964, challenged Lurleen Wallace for the governorship in 1966, his vote was negatively correlated with the 1964 Goldwater vote, in addition to its falling far short of its 1962 strength. Also in 1966, the vote of John Grenier, the guiding spirit of Alabama Republicanism, [2] was only slightly correlated with that of Goldwater in the case of the former's campaign against U.S. Senator John Sparkman. The pattern of both the Martin and Grenier votes in 1966 as well as the votes of subsequent Republican candidates in 1968 and 1972, therefore, had much more in common with the Nixon votes of 1960 and 1968 than with the Goldwater one of 1964 or the Nixon one of 1972.

Through the analysis of the regression coefficients in Table 14 it is possible to identify the common and different bases of the presidential and state-level votes. At the presidential level, the contrast between the social bases of the 1960 and 1964 votes was one of the sharpest in the South. Alabama's 1960 Republican presidential vote received strong positive contributions from both the traditionally Republican and the white collar sectors, while in 1964 both variables offered negative contributions. The patterns of the senatorial and gubernatorial votes generally had more in common with the 1960 pattern than with the 1964 one, especially in the case of Martin's gubernatorial vote. Here, the contributions of both traditionally Republican and white collar sectors were nearly as high as they had been for the 1960 presidential vote.

In the case of Grenier's senatorial vote, the contributions of both traditionally Republican and white collar sectors were lower than those for Martin's vote. However, the most curious difference between the two votes is the strength of the black belt contribution to Martin's vote in contrast to the Grenier one. By 1966, this variable, the proportion Negro in the population, had become difficult to use in aggregate analysis because of the problem of determining whether it referred to white or Negro voting behavior. Consequently, it is important to control Negro voting registration, as in Table 15.

Clearly, the greatest difference between the Martin and Grenier voting coalitions was their divergent racial polarizations. Black belt whites abandoned the Republican gubernatorial candidate and rallied around the Wallace standard, as might be expected, while Negro voters appeared to choose Martin. The opposite pattern prevailed in the senatorial contest as the black belt whites stayed with Grenier but the Negroes apparently opted for Senator Sparkman. This represents yet another illustration of the relative instability of the black belt.

The 1966 decline in Republican strength from 1964 is of the utmost importance to the long-term trend of Alabama Republicanism. In 1962 Grenier became state Republican chairman after the Young Republicans toppled the patronage-oriented incumbent party leadership.[3] Subseq-

TABLE 14

REGRESSION COEFFICIENTS FOR REPUBLICAN PRESIDENTIAL VOTES SINCE 1960 and SENATORIAL AND GUBERNATORIAL VOTES SINCE 1962

State		a	b_{40}	b_n	b_w	R
Alabama County Data (n=67)						
1960 Presidential	(Nixon)	-.01	.93	.30	.66	.83
1962 Senatorial	(Martin)	.31	.20	.32	.16	.42
1964 Presidential	(Goldwater)	.76	-.12	.14	-.30	.40
1966 Gubernatorial	(Martin)	-.05	.79	.23	.57	.71
1966 Senatorial	(Grenier)	.22	.44	.05	.27	.58
1968 Presidential	(Nixon)	-.05	.50	.00	.37	.84
1968 Senatorial	(Hooper)	-.10	.48	.08	.69	.65
1972 Presidential	(Nixon)	.94	.00	-.12	-.40	.43
1972 Senatorial	(Blount)	.24	.37	.02	.17	.60
Georgia County Data (n=159)						
1960 Presidential	(Nixon)	.11	.40	-.09	.58	.50
1964 Presidential	(Goldwater)	.42	.05	.32	.10	.42
1966 Gubernatorial	(Callaway)	.05	.18	.16	.89	.56
1968 Presidential	(Nixon)	.12	.24	-.18	.51	.68
1968 Senatorial	(Patton)	-.01	.13	-.02	.56	.55

1970 Gubernatorial (Suitt)	.11	.28	-.17	.68	.66
1972 Presidential (Nixon)	.93	-.15	-.23	-.18	.58
1972 Senatorial (Thompson)	.35	.12	-.08	.21	.29
Mississippi County Data (n=82)					
1960 Presidential (Nixon)	-.01	.75	.13	.57	.62
1963 Gubernatorial (Phillips)	.12	1.48	.11	.50	.52
1964 Presidential (Goldwater)	.82	-1.84	.18	.22	.66
1966 Senatorial (Walker)	.26	-.79	-.05	.22	.16
1967 Gubernatorial (Phillips)	-.04	.55	.27	.68	.66
1968 Presidential (Nixon)	-.02	.38	.03	.42	.65
1972 Presidential (Nixon)	1.05	-.75	-.52	-.06	.87
1972 Senatorial (Carmichael)	.24	-1.23	-.05	.78	.42
South Carolina County Data (n=46)					
1960 Presidential (Nixon)	-.12	-.20	.46	1.58	.67
1962 Senatorial (Workman)	-.08	-.35	.38	1.32	.66
1964 Presidential (Goldwater)	.20	-.08	.42	.81	.58
1966 Senatorial (Parker)	.50	-.04	-.14	.13	.39
1966 Senatorial (Thurmond)	.59	-.35	-.13	.32	.48
1966 Gubernatorial (Rogers)	.27	-.18	.06	.45	.30
1968 Presidential (Nixon)	.19	-.43	-.15	.87	.70
1968 Senatorial (Parker)	.39	-.10	-.21	.21	.60
1970 Gubernatorial (Watson)	.30	-.30	.01	.55	.38
1972 Presidential (Nixon)	.92	-.12	-.48	-.10	.87
1972 Senatorial (Thurmond)	.74	-.10	-.30	.01	.72

TABLE 14 - CONTINUED

State	a	b_{40}	b_n	b_w	R
Louisiana Parish Data (n=64)					
1960 Presidential (Nixon)	.05	-.24	-.18	.69	.36
1962 Senatorial (O'Hearn)	-.09	-.50	.54	.76	.49
1964 Presidential (Goldwater)	.54	-1.02	.51	.14	.52
1964 Gubernatorial (Lyons)	-.26	.18	.43	1.37	.71
1968 Presidential (Nixon)	-.01	.24	-.05	.61	.75
1972 Presidential (Nixon)	.88	-.27	-.44	.03	.70
1972 Senatorial (Toledano)	.04	.10	-.04	.41	.70
1972 Gubernatorial (Treen)	.28	-1.02	.15	.76	.51

Legend:

a   = Y intercept
b_{40} = Coefficient of proportion Republican, 1940
b_n = Coefficient of proportion Negro, 1960
b_w = Coefficient of proportion white collar, 1960
R   = Multiple correlation coefficient

uently, he became chairman of the draft Goldwater movement in Alabama, southern regional director of the Goldwater for President drive, and after the Senator's nomination, executive director of the Republican National Committee. For Grenier and his associates, the nomination of a states' rights Republican presidential candidate in 1964 was an important, indeed crucial requisite for the building of a strong Republican party in Alabama. The Ripon Society authors write:

> Only such a candidate could galvanize the anti-civil rights sentiment of the white Alabamians and produce a massive Republican presidential victory. Such a victory would be necessary to shake the century-long Democratic loyalties of Alabama whites. Conveniently, Arizona Senator Barry Goldwater fit to a tee the prescription of the Republicans in Alabama. His states' rights doctrines and evangelic conservatism were music to the ears of enraged white Alabamians . . . Many youthful southern Republican Chairmen saw Goldwater's candidacy as an ideal means of drawing in Republican recruits and of shaking lifelong Democratic voting patterns.[4]

This strategy was a failure because of the special condition of the politics of protest in Alabama — its lack of institutionalization and consequent instability. The politics of protest is not unknown to this state. However, its course has been severely affected by the posture of George Wallace. Political protest and electoral stability can co-exist if the protest is institutionalized within the established parties. Indeed, this is a legitimate function of political parties in America, especially for the out-party.

In Alabama, this clearly has not occurred. The Republicans have benefitted from protest only to the extent that Wallace has permitted. In 1962 Martin rode a wave of protest which became an important ingredient in the nomination and deep South landslide of Senator Barry Goldwater. In 1966, this wave, although still present, was no longer Martin's. In the 1966 senatorial contest John Grenier tried to ride the same wave of protest but received relatively small support from the white collar sector.

Nevertheless, in spite of the differences between the candidacies of Martin and Grenier, both received support from the white collar sector. Its stronger support for Martin indicates its stable Republican tendency in the face of the Wallace appeal. The differing strengths of the white collar contributions to the Martin and Grenier votes in 1966 reflect the different contexts in which the two Republican candidates operated. That the white collar population was relatively more disposed to Martin than Grenier reflects the appeals and strengths of their opponents, Lurleen Wallace and John Sparkman. Unable to succeed himself, nor able to force the Legislature to alter the state constitution to permit his serving two consecutive terms, Wallace ran his wife, Lurleen, for the governorship. The credibility of an administration headed by Governor and Mr. Wallace played some part in the white collar sector's strong support for Martin. In addition, and perhaps more importantly, Wallace's likely chief opponent in 1966, Ryan DeGraffenried, was killed in a plane crash early in the primary election campaign. Of DeGraffenried, Marshall Frady writes: "he had been steadily and quietly building support throughout the state during Wallace's four years at the capitol and had behind him the newspapers, big business, the city politicians, and educational leaders-the establishment coalition."[5] In short, Wallace was not the first and enthusiastic choice of the sort of people who might be expected to represent the white collar sector. In contrast, Senator Sparkman still had a following here. Despite these differences, however, what is important to notice is that while the contributions of other groups varied, that of the white collar sector remained a consistent Republican resource, as it had been prior to 1964.

The expectation that the white collar sector is a basis for the institutionalization of Republicanism, even in Alabama, is further supported by the 1968 election for U.S. senator. Senator Lister Hill retired, providing the Republicans the advantage of facing a non-incumbent. Their candidate, Perry Hooper, polled only 24 per cent of the vote but at the same time nearly doubled the white collar support which Nixon polled in the presidential contest. Undoubtedly, Wallace's presidential candidacy served to suppress the Nixon vote in all sectors of the state.

The 1970 general election provided a telling commentary on the dominance of Wallace in Alabama and the relative feebleness of the Republican party here. The Republicans did not even contest the governorship, leaving the field to Wallace who won another term handily over two independent, largely liberal and black candidates. The major Alabama election of that year was the run-off Democratic primary election in which Wallace defeated incumbent Governor Albert Brewer, who had succeeded to the governorship upon the death of Lurleen Wallace in 1968. Brewer projected an image of moderation and sound administration, in contrast to the stridency, protest, and neo-Populism associated with a Wallace candidacy. Thus, Brewer drew upon the same forces as DeGraffenried four years previous, forces which would otherwise be Republican-leaning in the context of emerging southern political patterns. At the state level in Alabama, the Republican party responds, rather than innovates.

The 1972 U.S. Senate contest in Alabama held forth as much promise for Republican hopes as any in the deep South and yet ended in disappointment. Former Postmaster-General Winton Blount challenged veteran U.S. Senator John Sparkman and ended up polling only 32 per cent of the vote at the same time that President Nixon polled 72 per cent. Indeed, the expectation of the Nixon landslide was one reason Republicans had such hopes in the election for U.S. senator and waged an extremely vigorous campaign. Sparkman was advantaged by the issue of his seniority and its meaning for the welfare of Alabama together with Governor Wallace's endorsement of his candidacy. Moreover, Blount's wealth became a liability to his image. Governor Wallace was said to sneer at the Republican candidate's wealth, his large Montgomery estate, and wonder as well "how a man who had air-conditioned stables for his horses could be aware of the needs of the common man."[6] Again, this illustrates the degree to which Wallace's stance is the key to the Alabama electorate.

Georgia

In 1966 Georgia experienced its first serious state-wide inter-party competition since Reconstruction in U.S. Representative Howard "Bo" Callaway's race for governor. Callaway, a one-term congressman, nearly reached the governor's chair; he polled a plurality, but not a majority of the ballots, as required by the state constitution, in a three-way contest. In the absence of a majority, the overwhelmingly Democratic Georgia Legislature selected Lester Maddox, the Democratic nominee, to be governor.

The confusion in Georgia politics in 1966 stemmed from the occurrence of the unexpected. First, it was never expected that Lester Maddox, who had played on the fringes of Democratic politics for some time, would emerge victorious in the run-off Democratic gubernatorial primary. In the first primary, on September 14, 1966, the two moderate Democratic candidates polled more votes than the four segregationist ones, including Maddox, in spite of the fact that the balloting occurred soon after the Atlanta race riots. It is rumored that Callaway partisans voted for Maddox in the run-off primary on the expectation that he would be the easier Democrat to beat in the general election.[7] Secondly, the write-in campaign on behalf of Ellis Arnall, former governor and Maddox's opponent in the second primary, was surprisingly successful in the general election, garnering about 60,000 votes. This write-in campaign was aimed at white liberals and Negroes, and provided the margin which precluded either major party candidate from securing a majority in the close election.

TABLE 15

REGRESSION COEFFICIENTS FOR REPUBLICAN GUBERNATORIAL AND SENATORIAL VOTES, 1965-1970, CONTROLLING NEGRO VOTER REGISTRATION

State	a	b_{40}	b_n	b_w	b_r	R
Alabama						
1966 Gubernatorial	.04	.67	-.25	.45	.65*	.75
1966 Senatorial	.18	.49	.28	.32	-.30*	.60
1968 Senatorial	-.11	.50	.15	.71	-.09**	.65
Georgia						
1966 Gubernatorial	.04	.18	.21	.91	-.10*	.56
1968 Senatorial	-.01	.14	.00	.57	-.05**	.56
1970 Gubernatorial	.11	.28	-.20	.67	.05**	.66
Mississippi						
1966 Senatorial	.30	-1.34	-.28	.20	.37***	.33
1967 Gubernatorial	-.01	.25	.14	.67	.20***	.69

South Carolina

	a	b_{40}	b_n	b_w	b_r	R
1966 Senatorial	.49	.01	-.09	.15	-.10*	.40
1966 Senatorial	.58	-.22	.00	.37	-.24*	.53
1966 Gubernatorial	.27	-.20	.04	.44	.04*	.30
1968 Senatorial	.36	.04	.02	.30	-.32**	.63
1970 Gubernatorial	.28	-.23	.12	.59	-.15**	.39

Louisiana - no statewide Republican candidates, 1965-1970

Legend:

a	=	Y intercept
b_{40}	=	Coefficient of proportion Republican, 1940
b_n	=	Coefficient of proportion Negro in population, 1960
b_w	=	Coefficient of proportion white collar, 1960
b_r	=	Coefficient of proportion Negro among registered voters
R	=	Multiple correlation coefficient

*	1967 voter registration data used
**	1968 voter registration data used
***	1966 voter registration data used

During recent years, the center of Georgia Republicanism has shifted from the rural areas in the Appalachians north of Atlanta to the great metropolis and its suburbs itself, as well as to the other urban areas of the state. This Republican party was moderate in racial and economic matters, but in 1964 its leadership was toppled and replaced by Goldwater activists.[8] The period prior to 1964 had witnessed increasing white collar support for presidential Republicanism. In the 1964 vote this support dwindled and Republican leadership was taken by the rural counties. It was the strategy of Callaway to combine both elements in a winning coalition — the vote of the business oriented white collar counties and the rural ones. Indeed, the *Atlanta Constitution* castigated Callaway for electing "to ride the tiger that the old cynical Democrats rode when they used to saddle urban economic royalism on the state with the cinch of rural racist votes."[9]

Although he lost the election, Callaway's strategy was a success. Controlling Negro voter registration, as in Table 15, clearly reveals his coalition, Despite Maddox's rural appeal, Callaway was favored moderately by the black belt. The most impressive feature of his vote, however, was its white collar basis. Indeed, there is nearly a one-to-one relationship between the proportion Republican for governor in 1966 and the proportion white collar in 1960. There may be a paradox in the support given this Goldwater-oriented congressman by the white collar vote, which did not offer the same support for the Arizona senator. What these different patterns reflect, however, is that the rural counties dominated the state's Goldwater vote in 1964, but in 1966 the rural areas had a Democratic champion, Maddox. In this regard, the 1966 outcome in Georgia is similar to that of Alabama. The Callaway-Maddox battle of 1966 was a classic expression of the urban-rural battle in Georgia politics which hithertofore had been confined to the Democratic party.

It is remarkable that the Callaway strategy was as successful as it was. For Callaway's plight, as well as that of other southern Republican candidates in 1966, was how to contest Democratic hegemony without Goldwater on the ticket. The nemesis of these candidates was the lack of legitimacy of regular party Republicanism, especially in the rural areas. This was and may well remain a crucial problem for deep South Republicans to the extent that they fail to rekindle the Goldwater enthusiasm in their respective states.

There are indications that Callaway may not have perceived this problem until it overtook him. In the course of the gubernatorial campaign

Callaway discovered he could not count on support that he had taken for granted. It is reported that:

> Many who were once his political friends—powerful men, opinion-shapers on the right who counted him as a close and valuable ally when he was, as they are still, properly called neither a Democrat nor Republican but merely a protestor in national politics—now shunned him, feeling that he was making a giddy spectacle of himself.[10]

It is further reported that Callaway also failed to receive all the support which he had expected from other sources as well—in the event that there would be a run-off election and the choice would be between himself and Maddox. After the general election, when there was considerable speculation that the courts would never permit the legislature to select the governor, important business leaders and Ralph McGill, publisher of the *Atlanta Constitution,* came to the support of Maddox and not Callaway. McGill referred to the Republican candidate as a "sort of stainless steel young man, without emotions or feelings for people."[11] The newspaper failed to support him because, although it frowned upon both candidates, it felt that Maddox might provide an interregnum of farce but that Callaway could set up "better than twenty years of cold-hearted error."[12]

Callaway's campaign of 1966 ranks among the most vigorous of any deep South Republican during this period. He was representative of the new active deep South Republican in the 1960's in terms of his campaign strategy, his campaign problems, and, above all, in his political style. Opinion leaders—journalists and commentators—have been quick to point out a relative absence of difference between these new Republicans and the traditional Democrats. But their analyses are rooted in a concern for issues, usually racially-oriented ones. By contrast, the difference between Callaway and Maddox on the level of style was tremendous. Callaway, like many other new deep South Republicans, whirled into politics in the early 1960's, was a recent and exuberant convert from the Democratic to the Goldwater Republican party, was young, business-oriented, and ran an extensive and efficient campaign. Maddox, on the other hand, had a folksy style which was popular in small town and rural Georgia.

The 1970 gubernatorial election in Georgia again witnessed a serious Republican challenge which fell short of expectations. Nevertheless, support for the Republican candidate, Hal Suitt, was most pronounced in the white collar sector, as it was for Callaway. This points to the persistence of party support within a given social context even as the personalities, issues, and appeals of different campaigns and candidates change. And change there was between the Republican appeal in 1966 and 1970 in two important respects. First, Suitt, an Atlanta television news broadcaster until the announcement of his candidacy, was not a former conservative Democrat, as was Callaway before him or as was James Bentley, the man he soundly defeated in the Republican gubernatorial primary. Thus, Suitt's candidacy represents the development of an indigenous Republican cadre which is not dependent upon Democratic spin-offs nor upon the traditional Republican forces in the state. Secondly, the general election campaign was decidedly non-strident. Both candidates were known as moderates and both attempted to paint each other as liberals. The voters had a difficult time telling them apart.[13] In this situation, Georgia's traditional Democratic strength was sufficient to carry the election for Jimmy Carter.

Georgia is second only to South Carolina in holding forth Republican promise within the deep South. Yet a major Republican limitation emerged in the 1966 and 1970 gubernatorial campaigns. Despite the differences between Callaway and Suitt, there was a greater similarity in the way they were perceived by the electorate and similarly a common gulf between their respective images and those of their successful opponents, Maddox and Carter. In the 1970 gubernatorial campaign, Jimmy Carter was best characterized as a conservative-Populist. Although once considered a liberal because of his record as a state senator, he positioned himself to the right of former liberal Governor Carl Sanders in the crucial Democratic primary election and appealed to backers of Maddox and Wallace.[14] Despite the differences between Republican candidates, not only in Georgia but elsewhere in the South, they have not been able to capture the Populist spirit which is still important in these states and which is a foundation of the Maddox, Wallace, and Carter appeals.

The character of the emerging Republican-Democratic opposition in Georgia politics was displayed again in 1972 when Georgia Republicans, for the first time, seriously contested a U.S. senatorial election. Although a Republican did run against Senator Herman Talmadge four years earlier, in 1968, his campaign was lackluster and he polled only 23 per cent of the vote. The first task of Georgia Republicans in that year was the presidential contest. It was a different case in 1972. The Republican senatorial candidate, three-term Atlanta area congressman Fletcher Thompson, had two strong conditions in his favor—the anticipated landslide of President Nixon and the absence of an incumbent opposition candidate. Although

Thompson ran well, polling 46 per cent of the vote, he lost to Sam Nunn, a young, rural, conservative, state legislator. Thompson's major liability may have been his identification with the Atlanta area, in a state which routinely responds in terms of rural versus urban patterns, as well as the endorsement of his opponent by Senator Talmadge and Governor Wallace. The two previous serious Republican candidates, Callaway and Suitt, were similarly more in tune with the suburban and country club Republican image than with the "wool hats." What is important about the 1972 senatorial outcome is that it indicates that there is still a Democratic future beyond the demise of powerful incumbent Democratic office holders.

In the context of deep South politics, two successive and vigorous Republican gubernatorial challenges as well as one campaign for the U.S. Senate are noteworthy developments. In each of these three major contests the Republican candidate has polled better than 40 per cent of the vote. Most significantly, these campaigns have been attended by an organizational infrastructure which persists. In the words of Numan V. Bartley.

> While distinctly a minority party, the G.O.P. seems to have established itself as a functional alternative to the Democratic rule. The party appears well financed, and it appeals to a substantial statewide following. Its organizational machinery, especially in urban areas, is generally more efficient and effective than that possessed by the Democrats. As an institutional foundation of Georgia politics, the one-party system no longer exists.[15]

The direction for possible future success for Georgia Republicanism seems to lie in achieving an improved reception beyond the white collar sector. There is evidence that this is in fact taking place. The regression coefficients of Table 14 point to a declining contribution of the white collar variable to the Republican vote at the same time that the height of the regression line, indicated by the y intercept, is on the rise. This indicates an increasing diffusion of Republican strength in the state.

Mississippi

As in Alabama, the institutionalization of Republicanism on the non-presidential level has been less than successful in Mississippi. This has occurred despite the efforts of Mississippi Republicans to offer the same appeals that Goldwater did. Undoubtedly, this preference for Democrats on the state level reflects, in part, the fact that they sufficiently capture the protest spirit which the Mississippi whites feel.

The extent of the Goldwater landslide of 1964 surprised even the Mississippi Republicans, who could have won the state's entire congressional delegation that year had they offered candidates for all of the seats. As it was, the only Republican who dared run for Congress, Prentiss Walker, was elected. Ironically, his was the only district in the nation which had been credited with fewer than two 1964 Republican National Convention delegates under the incentive system of representation based upon previous Republican voting strength.[16] Falsely encouraged by the 1964 result, he challenged Senator James Eastland in the 1966 election and received only 27 per cent of the vote.

Both the Goldwater and Walker votes demonstrated identical positive contributions from the white collar sector, which is an important point of convergence. Yet, in other major ways, these were quite dissimilar votes. Obviously, one great difference between the two votes was their respective magnitudes, a phenomenon well reflected in their respective "a" coefficients. Moreover, the contribution of the black belt to these two votes differed in direction; it was positive for Goldwater and negative for Walker. The racial polarization in the senatorial vote emerges clearly when controlling on the proportion Negro in the electorate, as in Table 15. Still, that Eastland held the greater strength in the black belt is not surprising. As Chairman of the Senate Judiciary Committee, he had become the foremost defender of the white South, one of the most intransigent of southern Democrats on the issues of race, and one of the most outspoken of critics of the U.S. Supreme Court's decisions of the 1950's and 1960's.[17]

Walker's 1966 campaign was only one part of the effort by Mississippi Republicans to challenge Democratic hegemony on the state level. The other part concerns the two gubernatorial campaigns of Rubell Phillips in 1963 and 1967. In contrast to the pattern of the 1964 and 1966 Republican votes, the Republican gubernatorial votes evidenced positive contributions from the traditionally Republican sector and much higher contributions from the white collar one.

Phillips' 1963 gubernatorial campaign was part of the pre-Goldwater kindling of deep South Republicanism. Polling 39 per cent of the vote, and following after the demonstration of deep South Republican strength in the 1962 senate contests elsewhere, he further encouraged the expectations of a durable realignment in the deep South. He waged a strident anti-civil rights campaign whose slogan was "KO the Kennedys."[18] His Democratic opponent, Paul Johnson, ran an arch-segregationist campaign and explicitly charged that a two-party system could work only to the advantage of Negroes. In 1967 Phillips ran again for the governorship, this time against Congressman John Bell Williams, who had been stripped of his seniority by House Democrats after he supported Goldwater for President. In this, his second try, Phillips appealed to the growing Negro electorate and to moderates, but his vote tally fell to 30 per cent.[19]

The astounding Mississippi presidential Republican votes in 1964 and 1972 reflect the white bloc vote and the politics of racial protest. This politics of monolithic protest has hindered the institutionalization of inter-party competition inasmuch as racism, as an organizing principle of politics, has been furthered best in the absence of serious two-party competition. In 1971 the Republicans did not even contest the gubernatorial election. Mississippi Democrats have argued successfully that their state did not need a two-party system and that the presence of this kind of competition could only serve to benefit Negroes. At the same time the Negro electorate has eschewed Republican appeals, and has furthered splinter Democratic parties in the state. In a word, the Republican party and the notion of inter-party competition lack legitimacy here.

The 1972 general election presented a strange twist in this tale of Mississippi Republicanism. The Republican candidate for U.S. senator, Gil Carmichael, received a strong vote for a Mississippi Republican, 39 per cent, against Senator James Eastland. Yet, every effort had been made by national Republicans to ignore and discourage his candidacy. This reached the ludicrous example of Carmichael's being kept off a platform in Jackson, Mississippi, from which Vice President Agnew was making a campaign speech. Carmichael had served Republican purposes well enough by running in the Republican gubernatorial primary against James Meredith, who had integrated the University of Mississippi in 1962. In the general election a serious Republican challenge to an incumbent and powerful southern senator was an embarrassment to the Nixon strategy of not offending such persons.[20] Even with this handicap, Carmichael did receive considerable support from the white collar sector, which indicates a persistent Republican proclivity despite the vagaries of presidential politics.

South Carolina

South Carolina Republicanism is unique in the deep South. Only in this state do Republican presidential voting patterns since 1960 evidence a durable realignment. Only this state illustrates the partisan conversion of successful, office-holding Democrats, such as Senator Strom Thurmond and former Congressman Albert Watson. These personal conversions are of the utmost importance for the durable reorientation of the South Carolina electorate and symbolize the institutionalization of protest within the Republican party. The joining of Thurmond's fortunes to those of the Republicans in the second part of the 1960's stands in marked contrast to politics in Alabama, where the state's leading politician, George Wallace, opted to act outside the two-party system during this period.

The stability of recent South Carolina presidential Republicanism and conversion of top Democrats have been supported by the development of a vigorous party organization. As the party grew in strength, vitality, and effectiveness, it also became lily-white. In shifting from a patronage centered organization to a vote seeking one, in the late 1950's and early 1960's, the new Republicans purged the Negro party officials. Thereafter, the party became the respectable white man's party and a vehicle for protest against the policies of the national Democrats.

The transfer of presidential to non-presidential voting patterns can be examined in the gubernatorial and senatorial elections of 1966 and 1968. In 1966 there were two senate contests. The Republicans nominated Marshall J. Parker to face Ernest P. Hollings for the short senate term. For the full term, Senator Strom Thurmond ran for the first time as a Republican and was challenged by Democratic state senator Bradley Morrah. In the gubernatorial race, the Republicans nominated state representative Joseph O. Rogers to challenge incumbent Governor Robert E. McNair. In 1968 there was a rematch of the Parker-Hollings contest.

The voting patterns in these state elections tend to reflect the presidential voting patterns, but in a muted form. The coefficients in Table 14 indicate that white collar Republicanism still prevailed in these elections, but not at the level that it had in the presidential elections. Although this still represents a limited institutionalization of white collar Republicanism, the same claim cannot be made for the black belt. This sector had offered strong support to the Republican presidential votes of 1960 and 1964 but its contribution was negative in three of the four state contests. The one instance in which it was slightly positive was in the vote for gubernatorial candidate Rogers. It is likely that this reflects the effects of support by Negroes, as the coefficients in Table 15 indicate.[21]

The 1968 senate contest was a disappointment to Republicans because

Parker had polled 49 per cent of the vote against Hollings in 1966 but his vote fell to 38 per cent in the rematch. This 1968 contest illustrates problems posed by the three-way presidential contest. Parker supported Nixon for President but courted the Wallace voters as well, saying that he could work with either a Nixon or Wallace administration, but definitely not a Humphrey one.[22] Parker's strategy was unsuccessful, however, and Wallace voters did not vote Republican for U.S. senator. This accounts, in part, for Parker's fall in strength from 1966 levels. In an additional respect, the Republican senatorial candidate was handicapped in his 1968 race because the greater campaign effort and resources went into the presidential contest. Despite the fact that Nixon won a plurality in 1968 in this state, the three-way presidential contest proved a disaster for state and local Republican candidates. Recent Republican gains in the state legislature were virtually wiped out.

More than in any other deep South state, inter-party competition has become institutionalized in South Carolina, although in an imperfect manner. This is reflected in the relatively high votes for Republican candidates for U.S. senator and governor and their consistently vigorous campaigns. In contrast to other states of the sub-region, a broad base is emerging which may be of benefit to Republican candidates in the future. For although white collar Republicanism is not as strong on this level as on the presidential one, the votes for senatorial and gubernatorial candidates are remaining fairly high for the deep South. In the other deep South states, the vote for Republican gubernatorial and senatorial candidates has usually been both smaller and more narrowly based in the white collar sector. In the South Carolina gubernatorial and senatorial votes, the class cleavage is not as narrow. This points to the diffusion of competition throughout the state.

This successful diffusion of competition reflects the fact that, unlike the states of Alabama and Mississippi, inter-party competition is legitimate in South Carolina. This is due both to the conversion of Senator Thurmond and the relatively moderate evolution of the state Democratic party. Senator Hollings and former Governor McNair are outstanding examples of a new breed of successful Democratic politicians in the deep South who do not owe their positions to intransigence on race issues. Thus, a durable Republican realignment is reflecting changes in the opposition party as well.

The 1970 gubernatorial election held special promise for South Carolina Republicans and was vigorously contested. The Republican candidate, Albert S. Watson, bore none of the handicaps which other South Carolina Republican challengers faced in 1966 and 1968. His opponent was not an incumbent, nor were there the distractions and division of resources which attend a presidential campaign. Watson himself enjoyed statewide visibility as the U.S. representative who switched to the Republican party, resigned his congressional seat, and was re-elected as a Republican after a heated campaign in 1965. In view of these several factors, Watson should have won the gubernatorial election in 1970. Instead, he lost, polling 46 per cent of the vote.

Unlike the situation in Georgia, there was a great gulf between the gubernatorial candidates in South Carolina in 1970. John West, the incumbent lieutenant governor and Democratic gubernatorial candidate, ran as a racial moderate, a position consistent with the tone of outgoing Governor McNair's administration. By contrast, Watson attempted to stimulate racial polarization in the state, a strategy he had practiced earlier in his successful congressional elections. In the opening television commercial of the 1970 campaign Watson used film clips of Negro rioters and warned against the "black bloc" vote.[23] The regression coefficients of Table 15 point to the racial polarization which ensued. Understandably, Democratic candidate West swept the Negro precincts, but in addition made heavy inroads among whites who were moderate on racial issues and who had voted for Nixon in 1968 as well as among textile workers who went for Wallace in 1968 but who were increasingly conscious of rising unemployment.[24]

In 1972 Strom Thurmond was re-elected to the U.S. Senate by a landslide vote of 64 per cent, surpassing his 1966 victory margin. Two features of this vote merit notice. First, victory itself would indicate the Senator's ability to withstand whatever resentment Wallace partisans might have held against him for his role in the Nixon campaign of 1968. In the period before it became apparent that Wallace would be a Democrat in 1972, such revenge was considered to be a distinct possibility. Secondly, the quality of Thurmond's vote in 1972 was unusual in view of its similarity to the Nixon vote in that year. The correlation between the two votes (.91) was the highest of any in the deep South for U.S. senator or governor and President in the post-1960 era. Thurmond's strength was state-wide as was Nixon's and received no relative appreciable contribution from the white collar sector. This finding is of critical importance to the theory of electoral realignment. Earlier, the analysis of presidential Republicanism indicated that South Carolina was the only deep South state which clearly underwent a broad electoral realignment in the 1960's. There was more continuity between successive pairs of presidential elections in this state than in any other in the sub-region. The fact that a non-presidential vote has reflected the presidential pattern, even as that presidential pattern shifted somewhat in 1972, is another important indicator of the unique realignment in South Carolina. Whether this pattern will hold for candidates other than Thurmond, and in other states as well, is an open question.

Louisiana

During the second half of the 1960's, state-wide inter-party competition was less prominent in Louisiana than in any other deep South state. From an organizational perspective, Louisiana Republicanism may have been the least well developed of any of these states. Party voter registration figures, which are a convenient index to party organizational vitality, reflect this lack of development. One estimate of party registration in the mid 1960's found only about 19,000 registered Republicans out of a total registration of about 1,200,000.[25] In early 1972, voter registration figures found only 36,050 Republicans as compared to 1,579,999 Democrats.[26] Of course, Republican candidates run better than these figures might indicate. But, they do not contest elections at the state-wide level on a regular basis, which is a central problem for Louisiana Republicanism. Non-presidential Republicanism here has been a disjointed and sometime affair.

Prior to 1972, Louisiana witnessed only two spirited statewide campaigns here – the 1962 senatorial campaign of Taylor W. O'Hearn and the 1964 gubernatorial campaign of Charlton Lyons, a wealthy Shreveport businessman, who polled a surprising 39 per cent of the vote against John J. McKeithan. The Lyons campaign represents the first serious statewide Republican campaign in Louisiana. Inasmuch as Louisiana holds its gubernatorial election in the spring of the year, this campaign and vote were important harbingers of the Goldwater appeal in the deep South. Indeed, Lyons campaigned as a staunch conservative and supporter of Senator Goldwater.[27] The Republicans did not contest the 1968 gubernatorial election, possibly because of the wide popularity of incumbent Governor McKeithan, nor the 1966 and 1968 U.S. senatorial elections. Thus, in an era when other deep South Republican parties were building organizations and contesting elections, a hiatus seems to have prevailed in Louisiana Republicanism.

The Republican potential in gubernatorial balloting was demonstrated again in 1972 when David C. Treen polled 43 per cent of the vote against Edwin Edwards. However, in the autumn general election, the Republican candidate for U.S. senator, Benjamin Toledano, received only 19 per cent of the vote. This low tally no doubt reflected the fact that four candidates contested the election, three of whom were considered serious contenders — Democratic nominee J. Bennett Johnston who won the election, former Governor McKeithan who ran as an independent, and Toledano. The opportunity provided by the death of incumbent Senator Ellender stimulated wider interest in the U.S. senatorial election than in the presidential one, whose outcome was a foregone conclusion.[28]

A persistent basis of Louisiana's non-presidential vote has been its positive support by the white collar sector. However, the contributions of the traditionally Republican and black belt sectors have been more variable. And, of course, the growth of Negro voter registration has made the situation all the more complicated. Both sizeable gubernatorial votes enjoyed positive support by the black belt while the low Republican votes for President in 1968 and U.S. senator in 1972 did not. This highlights the more narrow and concentrated basis for the smaller votes.

The pattern of the 1972 Republican gubernatorial vote in Louisiana merits notice as this represents the strongest Republican showing in Louisiana for a state-wide office. This vote was based in the white collar sector, whose leading counties are scattered in northern and southern Louisiana, and to a lesser extent was based as well in the black belt, which is disproportionately present in northern Louisiana. The positive correlation (.24) of the proportion Negro in 1960 and the proportion Republican for President in 1944 in comparison with its negative correlation with the 1940 presidential vote (-.03) points to the northern Louisiana location of the black belt and indirectly to the northern Louisiana basis for recent Republican voting. The 1944 Republican presidential vote had represented a shift to the northern parishes and away from the traditional Republican ones in southern Louisiana.

There is reason to expect that the institutionalization of protest in the Republican party in the northern parishes points to an emerging Republican resource. In recent years the northern parishes have registered nearly twice as many Republicans as the traditionally Republican southern parishes.[29] Despite this potential Republican resource, however, it is clear that new Republican registrations are no match for new Democratic ones.

Republican candidates who run well do so only by attracting even more Democrats than Republicans, at least as these are measured by party registration. It rakes a spirit of protest to vote against one's habitual party and Republicanism, here as well as elsewhere in the South, will depend upon this spirit.

Summary

The existence of serious inter-party competition has now been established, at least part of the time, in each of the five deep South states. This alone represents a major change and one impelled by the realignment in presidential voting. In most instances the pattern of these U.S. senatorial and gubernatorial votes has reflected, in general, the pattern of presidential Republicanism which prevailed for the past two decades with the exception of the 1964 and 1972 presidential elections.

Despite the differences in the appeals of the different Republican candidates, their basis of support in the white collar sector persisted in nearly every case. This pattern is the combined product of the saliency of economic class factors and the likely response of the sector least tied to the traditional Democratic politics of the South. Of course, support by the white collar sector is not sufficient to win or, indeed, even to run well. And the traditionally Republican sectors in these states are not sufficiently large to make much of a difference, even when their contributions are positive. Instead, it is outside of these two sectors that sizeable, though erratic gains in Republican voting have been recorded. Sometimes, this occurs in the black belt sector; sometimes it is reflected in a high and widespread Republican vote, indicated by the coefficient "a" or the y intercept, which transcends the white collar, black belt, and traditionally Republican sectors. Such a situation is quintessentially a protest one analogous to 1964 and 1972 presidential Republicanism.

Southern protest against national public policy and the evolution of the Democratic party is not new and has been a prominent theme of American politics since 1937. The ability of deep South Republicans to be the vehicle of this protest is limited largely by the posture of the southern Democratic parties and the character of their evolving realignment. Such dominant personages as Eastland, Wallace, and Thurmond, are still able to hold the rural votes in their states, and only one of these men is a Republican. This does not imply that the white collar sector is incapable of the same sort of protest. Indeed, it is. But, the protest of this sector is joined to the Republican party in a more durable fashion. The relatively high white collar coefficients point to this durability in the face of the decline of Republican strength outside this sector.

In the decade of the 1960's, a marked shift in the stance and orientation of some of the southern Democratic parties occurred. This is likely to lead to a more durable Republican voting pattern. Party realignment takes place in a system of interaction in which change in one party affects the character of change in the other. The Democratic parties in South Carolina, Georgia, and even Louisiana are much more moderate than they were a decade ago or are yet in Mississippi and perhaps Alabama. The race question is central to this change. The rapid recent enfranchisement of the Negro has led to the problem of a political strategy which is open to Negro participation and support without alienating the traditionally Democratic white vote. Recent Democratic governors of South Carolina, Georgia, and Louisiana have been successful in just this way which is a strong argument against the sometime notion of a future solid Republican South.

FOOTNOTES

1. Walter Dean Burnham, "The Alabama Senatorial Election of 1962: Return of Inter-Party Competition," *Journal of Politics*, XXVI (November, 1964), pp. 798-829.

2. John C. Topping, Jr., John R. Lazarek, and William H. Linder, *Southern Republicanism and and the New South* (Cambridge, Mass.: The Ripon Society, 1966), p. 29.

3. *Ibid.*

4. *Ibid.*

5. Marshall Frady, *Wallace* (Cleveland, Ohio: Meridian Books, 1968), p. 190.

6. *The New York Times*, November 8, 1972, p. 6.

7. *Atlanta Constitution*, November 3, 1966, p. 4.

8. Topping, *Southern Republicanism*, pp. 60-61.

9. *Atlanta Constitution*, November 3, 1966, p. 4.

10. Robert Sherrill, "Nixon's Man in Dixie," *The New York Times Magazine*, September 15, 1968, p. 47.

11. *The New York Times*, November 20, 1966, pp. 1, 84.

12. Sherrill, "Nixon's Man," p. 49.

13. *The New York Times*, November 4, 1970, p. 32.

14. *Congressional Quarterly Weekly Report*, Vol. 28, No. 39, (September 25, 1970), p. 2340.

15. Numan V. Bartley, *From Thurmond to Wallace* (Baltimore: The Johns Hopkins Press, 1970), p. 7.

16. Topping, *Southern Republicanism*, p. 75.

17. For a sharply etched portrait of Senator Eastland see Robert Sherrill, *Gothic Politics in the Deep South*, (New York: Grossman, 1968), ch. 7.

18. Topping, *Southern Republicanism*, p. 75.

19. It is likely that the effects of both the proportion of Negroes in the population and the proportion of Negroes among the registered electorate are distorted due to multicollinearity, not only in Mississippi, but in all deep South states.

20. *The Washington Post*, October 1, 1972, p. 5.

21. Here too the statistical effects of Negro voter registration are likely understated due to the problem of multicollinearity.

22. *The State* (Columbia, S.C.), October 31, 1968. It should be pointed out that Senator Hollings went one step further and said that although he felt obligated as a Democratic candidate to vote for Humphrey he thought he could work effectively in the Senate no matter which candidate for President was elected. *Ibid.*

23. *The New York Times,* November 4, 1970, p. 32.

24. *Ibid.*

25. Topping, *Southern Republicanism,* p. 68.

26. *Congressional Quarterly Weekly Report,* Vol. 30, No. 8, (February 19, 1972).

27. Perry H. Howard, "Louisiana: Resistance and Change," in William C. Havard (ed.), *The Changing Politics of the South* (Baton Rouge: Louisiana State University Press, 1972), pp. 564-565.

28. *The New York Times,* November 8, 1972, p. 11.

29. Howard, "Louisiana," p. 529.

Chapter VI

The Diffusion of Competition: The Rim South

Nineteen-seventy-two was a very good year for rim South Republicans who re-elected Republican U.S. senators in Texas and Tennessee and elected new Republican senators in Virginia and North Carolina, as well as a Republican governor in North Carolina. This continued a trend, first prominent in 1966, of greater electoral success in the rim South than in the deep South.

The substantial good fortunes of rim South Republicans in the years since 1966 suggest something of a paradox. For the 1964 Republican presidential vote here was not the electoral departure that it was in the deep South. Thus, where electoral patterns had been disturbed most in 1964, in the deep South, Republicans ran less well in the ensuing years; where electoral patterns had been disturbed least, in the rim South, Republican senators and governors were elected. This runs counter to what the Goldwater strategists' expectations of what a breakthrough on the presidential level of voting could mean for Republican voting at other levels. And even in the deep South, it was South Carolina, the most electorally stable of states since 1960, which actually elected a Republican at the state level.

Both the greater stability of the rim South presidential vote as well as the greater electoral success of senatorial and gubernatorial campaigns reflect the greater institutionalization of inter-party competition in the rim South. In addition, the individual campaigns reflect a greater plurality of options for Republican appeals in this sub-region than in the more monolithic deep South. This greater variability helps indicate the conditions conducive to party development and innovation.

The variance in this is important in its own right as an indicator of the likely future of non-presidential southern Republicanism, at least at the state office level. Yet, as Gerald M. Pomper pointed out, an analysis of electoral change must consider separately the power dimension and the electoral cleavage dimension. [1] Thus, from a realignment perspective, it is still the underlying social basis of the vote which must be probed. In particular, it is important to note what pattern of cleavages seems to predict electoral success in the rim South, especially given the wider range of appeals which have been employed by Republicans in this sub-region.

This stress on underlying electoral cleavages is also important in judging the effects of the 1964 Republican presidential vote on subsequent Republican development. Although the Republican vote in 1964 was more stable in the rim than the deep South, there were exceptions to this pattern, some of them very striking indeed, such as those of Florida and Arkansas. As in the deep South, then, there emerged two alternative patterns for the institutionalization of Republican competition.

In view of the greater electoral stability in these states it is not surprising that most of the Republican votes for senator and governor were well correlated with all the presidential votes, 1960-1972. Yet, there were exceptions to this tendency and in most instances these exceptions demonstrated high correlations with the 1960 and 1968 votes and low correlations with the 1964 and 1972 votes, or vice-versa. Thus, the basic alternative patterns for the Republican presidential vote are manifest again in some of these states beneath the presidential level. This lends support to the expectation that one alignment pattern might not definitely replace the other but that both could vary in an alternative fashion. The particular determinants of the correlations presented in Table 16 as well as their consequences in terms of victory or defeat are explored in the following state by state analysis.

Despite both the differential rates of electoral success and the patterns of electoral cleavage, it remains fundamentally important that vigorous inter-party competition has persisted. The contesting of elections, the building of party organizations, and the cultivation of the expectation in the electorate that Republicanism is an ordinary rather than extraordinary phenomenon has been no mean achievement. Moreover, it is an essential step toward the maintenance of responsibility in government.

The Institutionalization of Competition Since 1964

Tennessee

In the post-Civil War period, political cleavages in Tennessee coincided not with class or occupational divisions, but rather with geography — parts of eastern Tennessee were as staunchly Republican as parts of middle and western Tennessee were Democratic. These geo-political cleavages resulted from the presence of a slave economy in the western plantation sections and its absence in the eastern hill sections of the state. This eco-

TABLE 16
CORRELATIONS OF SELECTED REPUBLICAN SENATORIAL AND GUBERNATORIAL VOTES WITH REPUBLICAN PRESIDENTIAL VOTES SINCE 1960

State	Contest	r,1960	r, 1964	r, 1968	r, 1972
Tennessee					
1964 Senatorial	(Kuykendall v. Gore)	.93	.99	.86	.87
1964 Senatorial	(Baker v. Bass)	.93	.98	.88	.88
1966 Senatorial	(Baker v. Clement)	.89	.91	.89	.86
1970 Gubernatorial	(Dunn v. Hooker)	.91	.95	.86	.91
1970 Senatorial	(Brock v. Gore)	.87	.96	.79	.92
1972 Senatorial	(Baker v. Blanton)	.83	.82	.84	.85
North Carolina					
1962 Senatorial	(Greene v. Ervin)	.96	.85	.93	.38
1964 Gubernatorial	(Gavin v. Moore)	.91	.92	.84	.53
1966 Senatorial	(Shallcross v. Jordan)	.84	.83	.78	.46
1968 Gubernatorial	(Gardner v. Scott)	.80	.86	.78	.65
1958 Senatorial	(Somers v. Ervin)	.94	.87	.90	.46
1972 Gubernatorial	(Holshouser v. Bowles)	.90	.87	.87	.59
1972 Senatorial	(Helms v. Galifianakis)	.46	.60	.47	.75

TABLE 16 - CONTINUED

State	Contest	r, 1960	r, 1964	r, 1968	r, 1972
Arkansas					
1962 Gubernatorial	(Ricketts v. Faubus)	.72	.18	.79	.26
1962 Senatorial	(Jones v. Fulbright)	.58	.59	.54	.49
1964 Gubernatorial	(Rockefeller v. Faubus)	.64	.06	.70	.07
1966 Gubernatorial	(Rockefeller v. Johnson)	.55	.13	.52	.13
1968 Gubernatorial	(Rockefeller v. Crank)	.60	.21	.56	.18
1968 Senatorial	(Bernard v. Fulbright)	.69	.32	.68	.44
1970 Gubernatorial	(Rockefeller v. Bumpers)	.19	.32	.10	-.04
1972 Gubernatorial	(Blaylock v. Bumpers)	.72	.12	.70	.21
1972 Senatorial	(Babbitt v. McClellan)	.51	-.10	.64	.04
Florida					
1962 Senatorial	(Rupert v. Smathers)	.86	-.09	.90	-.23
1964 Senatorial	(Kirk v. Holland)	.70	.22	.76	-.12
1964 Gubernatorial	(Holley v. Burns)	.81	.30	.76	-.12
1964 Gubernatorial	(Kirk v. High)	.56	.19	.52	.37
1968 Senatorial	(Gurney v. Collins)	-.17	.68	-.35	.78
1970 Gubernatorial	(Kirk v. Askew)	.73	-.04	.70	-.08
1970 Senatorial	(Cramer v. Chiles)	.88	-.05	.90	-.11

Virginia

1961 Gubernatorial	(Pearson v. Harrison)	.46	-.24	.52	-.02
1964 Senatorial	(May v. Byrd)	.28	-.16	.57	.20
1965 Gubernatorial	(Holton v. Godwin)	.48	-.12	.72	.28
1966 Senatorial	(Ould v. Spong)	.55	.04	.82	.43
1966 Senatorial	(Traylor v. Byrd)	.26	-.23	.23	-.24
1969 Gubernatorial	(Holton v. Battle)	.68	.29	.76	.67
1970 Senatorial	(Garland v. Rawlings, Byrd)	.31	-.18	.62	.17
1972 Senatorial	(Scott v. Spong)	.40	.61	.34	.69

Texas

1960 Senatorial	(Tower v. Johnson)	.96	.80	.84	.63
1961 Senatorial	(Tower v. Blakley)	.83	.78	.80	.53
1962 Gubernatorial	(Cox v. Connally)	.83	.88	.78	.69
1964 Gubernatorial	(Crichton v. Connally)	.78	.94	.70	.63
1964 Senatorial	(Bush v. Yarborough)	.84	.96	.80	.75
1966 Gubernatorial	(Kennerly v. Connally)	.63	.74	.63	.50
1966 Senatorial	(Tower v. Carr)	.76	.83	.74	.68
1968 Gubernatorial	(Eggers v. Smith)	.71	.74	.75	.54
1970 Gubernatorial	(Eggers v. Smith)	.68	.71	.70	.49
1970 Senatorial	(Bush v. Bentsen)	.72	.77	.78	.58
1972 Gubernatorial	(Grover v. Briscoe)	.56	.64	.54	.55
1972 Senatorial	(Tower v. Sanders)	.76	.74	.78	.84

nomic division was the basis for Civil War era arguments about where political allegiance belonged — with the Union or the Confederacy. In this manner the heritage of Republican and Democratic loyalties began. In later decades the regional cleavage was reinforced by the political strategies of the Republicans in the east and the Democrats in the west not to challenge each other within their respective sections. V.O. Key, Jr. summed up this Tennessee tradition in suggesting that "Tennessee in a sense has not one one-party system but rather two one-party systems."[2]

Thus, the essential character of past Tennessee Republicanism is that it was long established or institutionalized, and that it was unambitious.[3] Both of these factors account for the marked stability of the Tennessee Republican vote, which exceeds that of any other southern state. Given this background, serious statewide Republican candidates in Tennessee have had to hold their support in the east and to build new support in other sections. The traditionally Republican sector, by itself, has never been sufficiently strong to challenge hegemony on the state level. Nixon succeeded in gathering a Republican plurality in 1960 by going beyond the traditionally Republican sector and polling support in the black belt. And even the Republican plurality in the three-way contest of 1968 depended upon broader bases than the traditionally Republican sector alone.

After the 1970 elections, Tennessee became the first southern state to boast of Republicans occupying the governorship and both U.S. senate seats simultaneously. And in each of these winning instances, the candidates generated a broader basis of support than unsuccessful candidates had previously. In particular, each of their votes was characterized by a relatively strong contribution from the white collar sector.

The non-presidential Republican advance in Tennessee was first manifest in 1966 when Howard H. Baker, Jr. was elected to the U.S. Senate polling 56 per cent of the vote. Baker had run for the Senate previously, in 1964. In his first and losing campaign, the pattern of his vote closely paralleled that of Goldwater's presidential vote. The civil rights overtones of that election year cost the Republican senatorial candidate many votes. His opponent for the two-year term, Ross Bass, benefited from strong Negro support for President Johnson. Moreover, Bass had been one of the few southern congressmen to vote for the 1964 Civil Rights Act.[4] Although defeated, Baker did run well, leading Goldwater and polling more than 48 per cent of the vote.

Baker's 1964 vote received strong contributions from the traditionally

Republican and black belt sectors, as Table 17 indicates. Since voter registration data are not available by race for 1964 and 1966 in Tennessee, a
precise test of the contributions of white and Negro black belt voters is not
possible. However, given the circumstances of the 1964 presidential election, the high correlation between the presidential and senatorial votes, the
similarity of the regression coefficients for both votes, and Bass' standing
among Negroes, it is reasonable to expect that the strong black belt contribution to Baker's vote was a predominantly white vote.

In the election for the other senate seat, Republican Dan Kuykendall
challenged incumbent Senator Albert Gore. The pattern of Kuykendall's
losing vote resembled Baker's, with the exception that Baker did slightly
better among white collar voters.[5]

In his second and successful senate election contest, in 1966, Baker first
faced a challenge in the primary election. He won a landslide victory in the
Republican senatorial primary against an opponent who had managed the
1964 Goldwater campaign in the state. On the Democratic side, Governor
Frank Clement upset Senator Ross Bass in the senatorial primary, in a rematch of their 1964 primary fight. In the general election campaign, both
candidates ran as moderates, taking similar positions on most issues, and
both appealed for the Negro vote.[6]

Baker polled a decisive majority over Clement by forging a coalition
unique in recent Tennessee politics. In contrast to the pattern of this 1964
vote, Baker's 1966 vote exhibited a decline in the contribution of the traditionally Republican and black belt sectors and a sharp increase in the
support offered by the white collar sector. Indeed, its contribution reached
a higher level than it had previously in Tennessee for any of the contests,
presidential included. These patterns were continued in Baker's 1972 re-
election, in which he polled 62 per cent of the vote. This new Republican
coalition in Tennessee is important because it represents the decline of the
traditional geo-political cleavage and the ascendancy of a new one, the
white collar basis for Republicanism, which is consistent with the pattern
of emerging electoral cleavages elsewhere in the South. Moreover, this is
also the pattern predicted by the theory of the New Deal electoral realignment.

The extension of Republican competition across Tennessee, which
Baker's vote represented, was also accomplished by Winfield Dunn, who
defeated John Jay Hooker for governor, and by U.S. Representative William E. Brock III, who defeated incumbent U.S. Senator Albert Gore.[7]

TABLE 17

REGRESSION COEFFICIENTS FOR REPUBLICAN PRESIDENTIAL, SENATORIAL, AND GUBERNATORIAL VOTES, 1960-1972

State	a	b_{40}	b_n	b_w	R
Tennessee County Data (n=95)					
1960 Presidential (Nixon)	.17	.86	.29	.07	.93
1964 Presidential (Goldwater)	.07	.81	.65	.02	.92
1964 Senatorial (Kuykendall)	.07	.86	.69	.05	.92
1964 Senatorial (Baker)	.07	.84	.61	.12	.92
1966 Senatorial (Baker)	.17	.69	.35	.37	.88
1968 Presidential (Nixon)	.05	.82	.05	.16	.94
1970 Senatorial (Brock)	.10	.76	.68	.22	.87
1970 Gubernatorial (Dunn)	.06	.75	.54	.43	.90
1972 Presidential (Nixon)	.45	.44	.30	.14	.81
1972 Senatorial (Baker)	.25	.52	.25	.44	.82
North Carolina County Data (n=100)					
1960 Presidential (Nixon)	.29	.52	-.37	.39	.92
1962 Senatorial (Greene)	.12	.65	-.28	.36	.93
1964 Presidential (Goldwater)	.24	.41	-.06	.31	.78
1964 Gubernatorial (Gavin)	.16	.52	-.16	.49	.84
1966 Senatorial (Shallcross)	.23	.55	-.06	.18	.80

1968 Presidential	(Nixon)	.24	.45	-.39	.39	.92
1968 Gubernatorial	(Gardner)	.36	.34	-.15	.18	.77
1968 Senatorial	(Somers)	.23	.57	-.24	.22	.92
1972 Presidential	(Nixon)	.70	-.03	-.16	.13	.38
1972 Senatorial	(Helms)	.52	.14	-.08	.00	.39
1972 Gubernatorial	(Holshouser)	.38	.36	-.24	.25	.82
Arkansas County Data (n=75)						
1960 Presidential	(Nixon)	.16	.83	-.04	.32	.84
1962 Senatorial	(Jones)	.07	.44	.11	.38	.61
1962 Gubernatorial	(Ricketts)	-.05	.55	.04	.60	.83
1964 Presidential	(Goldwater)	.23	.33	.24	.28	.48
1964 Gubernatorial	(Rockefeller)	.11	.46	.05	.66	.73
1966 Gubernatorial	(Rockefeller)	.05	.62	.29	.96	.75
1968 Presidential	(Nixon)	.07	.65	-.12	.40	.91
1968 Gubernatorial	(Rockefeller)	.07	.54	.24	.90	.71
1968 Senatorial	(Bernard)	.30	.41	.05	.05	.60
1970 Gubernatorial	(Rockefeller)	-.04	.65	.51	.39	.80
1972 Presidential	(Nixon)	.65	.12	-.01	.06	.28
1972 Gubernatorial.	(Blaylock)	.17	.45	.04	-.08	.71
1972 Senatorial	(Babbitt)	.30	.24	-.20	.21	.74
Virginia County and City Data (n=130)						
1960 Presidential	(Nixon)	.33	.46	-.08	.20	.59
1961 Gubernatorial	(Pearson)	.21	.43	-.24	.13	.69
1964 Presidential	(Goldwater)	.46	.05	.06	-.04	.15

TABLE 17 - CONTINUED

State		a	b_{40}	b_{ln}	b_w	R
1964 Senatorial	(May)	.25	.08	-.36	-.06	.74
1965 Gubernatorial	(Holton)	.28	.32	-.42	.20	.81
1966 Senatorial	(Ould)	.39	.26	-.47	-.08	.84
1966 Senatorial	(Traylor)	.23	.37	.03	.05	.46
1968 Presidential	(Nixon)	.37	.26	-.32	.16	.80
1969 Gubernatorial	(Holton)	.45	.16	-.15	.13	.59
1970 Senatorial	(Garland)	.27	.14	-.41	-.19	.81
1972 Presidential	(Nixon)	.79	-.06	-.24	-.08	.49
1972 Senatorial	(Scott)	.61	.04	.09	-.16	.26
Texas County Data (n=254)						
1960 Presidential	(Nixon)	.28	.33	-.16	.42	.46
1960 Senatorial	(Tower)	.16	.39	-.13	.46	.56
1961 Senatorial	(Tower)	.17	.60	-.13	.54	.63
1962 Gubernatorial	(Cox)	.23	.32	-.13	.45	.45
1964 Presidential	(Goldwater)	.26	.20	.01	.40	.35
1964 Senatorial	(Bush)	.22	.22	-.11	.45	.40
1964 Gubernatorial	(Crichton)	.07	.21	-.01	.34	.43
1966 Gubernatorial	(Kennerly)	.04	.23	-.01	.39	.55
1966 Senatorial	(Tower)	.27	.30	-.04	.59	.49
1968 Presidential	(Nixon)	.19	.39	-.31	.40	.66

	a	b40	bn	bw	R
1968 Gubernatorial (Eggers)	.10	.29	-.15	.67	.54
1970 Gubernatorial (Eggers)	.10	.34	.01	.64	.62
1970 Senatorial (Bush)	.12	.33	-.01	.61	.57
1972 Presidential (Nixon)	.66	.08	-.13	.09	.22
1972 Gubernatorial (Grover)	.10	.16	.17	.69	.47
1972 Senatorial (Tower)	.44	.21	-.16	.25	.45
Florida County Data (n=67)					
1960 Presidential (Nixon)	.08	1.02	.14	.36	.84
1962 Senatorial (Rupert)	-.12	.78	.03	.42	.90
1964 Presidential (Goldwater)	.61	-.02	-.10	-.16	.17
1964 Senatorial (Kirk)	.05	.46	.04	.42	.76
1964 Gubernatorial (Holley)	.18	.51	.05	.22	.73
1966 Gubernatorial (Kirk)	.56	.35	-.09	-.13	.53
1968 Presidential (Nixon)	-.16	.96	.04	.69	.85
1968 Senatorial (Gurney)	.87	.00	-.21	-.54	.50
1970 Gubernatorial (Kirk)	.24	.63	.17	.01	.60
1970 Senatorial (Cramer)	.08	.78	.04	.39	.79
1972 Presidential (Nixon)	1.06	-.09	-.44	-.46	.69

Legend:

a = Y intercept

b40 = Coefficient of proportion Republican, 1940

bn = Coefficient of proportion Negro, 1960

bw = Coefficient of proportion white collar, 1960

R = Multiple correlation coefficient

The Republican gubernatorial victory was abetted by two circumstances. The first is that Dunn, while relatively unknown on a statewide basis, made his home in Memphis, in western Tennessee, which is traditionally Democratic region. He won the Republican gubernatorial primary on the strength of his considerable support in this city and surrounding Shelby county.[8] This support, added to the traditionally Republican support of eastern Tennessee, provided the combination of ingredients necessary for victory in the general election.The second circumstance was that his opponent, Hooker, had a definitely liberal appeal and liberalism was not favored by Tennessee voters in 1970.[9]

While the gubernatorial contest pitted a Democratic candidate with a general liberal appeal against a Republican opponent whose ideological stance was not very well defined, the issues in the U.S. senatorial election were more clearly delineated. Reg Murphy and Hal Gulliver write that Brock used three issues against Senator Gore—issues that were a liability for Gore in 1970. These included Gore's votes against confirmation of Judges Haynsworth and Carswell to the Supreme Court, southern white resentment against the prospect of forced busing to achieve racial integration of the schools, and Gore's opposition to the Dirksen prayer-in-the-schools amendment to the U.S. Constitution.[10] With such issues, Brock was able to build a coalition of traditional Republicans and usually Democratic conservatives. The contribution of the later group to Brock's vote is reflected in the regression coefficients which indicate a larger contribution of the black belt sector and a lower contribution of the white collar sector than had been the case for Baker's 1966 and 1972 votes or for Dunn's 1970 vote.

North Carolina

Although the Republican candidates in Tennessee were in the conservative mold, they ran independently of, and despite, the Goldwater factor. This does not hold for Republican candidates in North Carolina in the post-Goldwater period who consciously attempted to employ the Goldwater appeal in their election campaigns. This represented a shift away from the moderate appeal projected by Robert Gavin, the unsuccessful 1964 gubernatorial nominee. By contrast, John S. Shallcross, the 1966 Republican candidate for U.S. senator, former U.S. Representative James C. Gardner, the 1968 Republican gubernatorial nominee, and Jesse A. Helms, who, in 1972, became the first Republican elected in this century to the

U.S. Senate from North Carolina, cultivated votes where first Goldwater and later Wallace ran well- in the eastern part of the state.

As in Tennessee, political cleavages in North Carolina have reflected historic regional differences, with the eastern counties voting strongly Democratic and the western mountain ones supporting the Republicans. Unlike Tennessee, however, these regional political distinctions have been eroding since Eisenhower's first campaign. Also, although the magnitude of the white collar contribution has been larger in North Carolina than in Tennessee, it has been declining since 1956. This may well be a reflection of the migration of Negroes into the southern metropolitan areas. The Republican problem is that decline in mountain Republican strength has not been compensated by a rising Republican strength in the white collar sector. It is this situation which may have prompted the Republicans to look elsewhere for votes.

In challenging incumbent Senator Everett Jordan, Shallcross' 44 per cent of the vote was a respectable showing inasmuch as his candidacy was almost an afterthought. In the winter of 1966, *Congressional Quarterly* anticipated that U.S. Representative James C. Gardner, the 1968 gubernatorial nominee, would be Jordan's challenger. The vast popularity of Senator Jordan led Gardner to opt for a congressional race instead. It was not until shortly before the deadline that Shallcross filed his candidacy.

North Carolina had experienced a slight electoral departure in 1964 and the Shallcross vote tended to resemble the 1964 one. Although he regained the support in the traditionally Republican sector which Goldwater lost, the contribution of the black belt to both was similar and the contribution of the white collar sector declined even further than it had for Goldwater. Thus, the slight departure from the 1960 pattern which the Goldwater vote pattern represented, was not reversed, in general, in 1966. If anything, the 1966 Republican senatorial vote represented a continued expression of the slight shifts wrought in 1964.

Both Goldwater and Shallcross received the same share of the vote in their respective contests. The strength of their votes was achieved through gains in formerly Democratic areas, in particular - the black belt. This lesson was not lost on gubernatorial candidate Gardner in 1968. Gardner's strategy was to ride the coattails of both Nixon and Wallace, in much the same spirit as Georgia's Callaway two years previous. Expecting to take

the Nixon vote easily, he campaigned extensively in the eastern part of the
state, where Negroes were more numerous, partisanship more Democratic, and Wallace support strongest. Both the strength of Gardner's
vote, 47 per cent, and the regression coefficients indicate that this strategy almost worked. Controlling Negro voter registration, as in Table 18,
washes away the negative contribution from the black belt revealed in
Table 17, and indicates a slight positive contribution from black belt
whites. Gardner's Democratic opponent, incumbent Lieutenant Governor
Robert W. Scott had the advantage of his incumbency and his family
name, his father having been a North Carolina governor.

In terms of personality, campaign strategy and campaign style, there
was much in common between Gardner of North Carolina and Callaway
of Georgia. Both were relatively new young men in politics who rode the
tide of southern resentment against the liberal national Democratic
administrations of the 1960's. Both used a single term in Congress as a
springboard, albeit futile, toward statewide campaigns. Both epitomised,
on the state contest level, what the Goldwater strategy had represented on
the presidential level - "hunting where the ducks are."

North Carolina Republicanism maintained a promising presence in
gubernatorial and U.S. senatorial elections throughout the 1960's. This
was certainly a two-party state at this level. Yet, it was not until 1972 that
Republicans scored their first gubernatorial and senatorial victories here.
Moreover, this is one of the few states in which the Nixon landslide may
have had some effect on the outcome of the state elections.

The election strategy of U.S. senatorial candidate Jesse Helms and
gubernatorial candidate James Holshouser was not fundamentally different from the losing strategies of Shallcross and Gardner in previous years.
Essentially, this meant pursuing a statewide majority by adding black belt
support in conservative eastern North Carolina to the substantial but
minority traditional Republican base in the western part of the state.

Several factors abetted Republican fortunes in North Carolina in 1972.
The clear ideological polarization in the senate election was one factor.
The McGovern presidential candidacy undoubtedly led to the defection of
many traditional southern Democrats. The Republican senatorial candidate, Helms, was in a good position to exploit this feeling inasmuch as he
was a staunch, even reactionary, conservative opposing a moderate to liberal Democrat, U.S. Representative Nick Galifianakis. The handicap
which this ideological polarization posed for the Democrat was reinforced

by his defeat of incumbent U.S. Senator Everett Jordan in the primary election. Undoubtedly, Republican voting came easily to many disappointed Jordan partisans. The regression coefficients for the Helms vote reflect these circumstances. The lack of relative support in the white collar sector and the unusually low support of the traditionally Republican sector, together with the high value of the y intercept, point to a broad basis of support in the state rather than the more narrowly bounded support of just the white collar and traditionally Republican sectors. This broad support brought Helms 54 per cent of the vote.

The major Republican advantage in the gubernatorial contest lay in the corruption charge which clouded the closing months of incumbent Democratic Governor Scott's administration. At issue was the financing of Scott's gubernatorial bid four years previous. Although Scott was unable to run again, the charges became a liability for Hargrove Bowles, who was Holshouser's Democratic opponent. Holshouser, a state representative and a former state Republican chairman, was very much in the same youthful mold as James Gardner, the 1968 gubernatorial nominee. The Holshouser-Bowles contest, however, lacked the ideological polarization of the Helms-Galifianakis one and the Republican gubernatorial vote assumed the more usual pattern of a basis in the traditionally Republican and white collar sectors.

These two elections in North Carolina in 1972 are important not only because of the dramatic and historic character of the Republican breakthrough, but because they reflect the two alternative types of Republican voting in the South. The analysis of the presidential vote demonstrated two types of southern Republican voting, that epitomised by the votes of 1952-1960 and 1968 as opposed to that epitomised by the 1964 and 1972 votes. That the gubernatorial and senatorial votes in North Carolina in 1972, for the most part, aligned with these two types respectively can be inferred by the correlations of Table 16. The gubernatorial vote was more highly correlated with the 1960-1968 presidential votes than with the 1972 one while the senatorial vote was more highly correlated with both the 1964 and 1972 presidential votes than with the 1960 and 1968 ones. Apparently, either type can point to the route to victory on the non-presidential level in this rim South state, depending largely on the opportunities which the opposition campaign represents.

TABLE 18

REGRESSION COEFFICIENTS FOR SELECTED REPUBLICAN
VOTES, CONTROLLING NEGRO VOTER REGISTRATION

State	a	b_{40}	b_n	b_w	b_r	R
North Carolina						
1966 Senatorial	.22	.56	.09	.24	-.31*	.81
1968 Senatorial	.22	.57	-.16	.24	-.15*	.92
1968 Gubernatorial	.35	.35	.02	.24	-.34*	.78
Virginia						
1961 Gubernatorial	.21	.43	-.64	.08	.70**	.74
1964 Senatorial	.25	.08	-.33	-.06	-.04**	.74
1965 Gubernatorial	.28	.32	-.44	.20	.02**	.81
1966 Senatorial (Ould)	.39	.26	-.42	-.07	-.10**	.84
1966 Senatorial (Traylor)	.23	.38	-.25	.02	.50**	.52

	a	b40	bn		bw	R
Florida						
1966 Gubernatorial	.54	.32	.18	-.07	-.40	.55
1968 Senatorial	.86	-.01	-.06	-.50	-.23	.50
1970 Gubernatorial	.22	.58	.55	.07	-.60***	.61
1970 Senatorial	.07	.73	.43	.45	-.61***	.80
Arkansas #						
1964 Presidential	.21	.35	.68	.32	-.70	.57
1964 Gubernatorial	.11	.45	-.19	.64	.39	.75

Tennessee, Texas - data not available for voter registration by race

Legend:

a	=	Y intercept
b40	=	Coefficient of proportion Republican, 1940
bn	=	Coefficient of proportion Negro, 1960
bw	=	Coefficient of proportion white collar, 1960
R	=	Multiple correlation coefficient

*   1967 data used
**   1964 data used
***   1968 data used
#   data not available since 1963

Arkansas

Aggressive Republicanism in Tennessee emerged out of the traditional Republican organization; in North Carolina it expanded with the forces of the Goldwater candidacy; in Arkansas, however, it was personified by the late Winthrop Rockefeller who guided it independently of the traditional Republican forces and kept it aloof from the conservative and racist appeals which swept the white South in the mid 1960's. In four successive elections between 1964 and 1970 Rockefeller was the Republican candidate for governor in his adopted state, losing to Orval Faubus in 1964, winning against Jim Johnson in 1966 and against Marion Crank in 1968, and finally, as an incumbent, losing badly to Dale Bumpers, a newcomer in state politics.

In 1964 both Rockefeller and Goldwater garnered 43 per cent of the vote but their bases of support differed. Ticket-splitting was widespread under the encouragement of organized groups such as Democrats for Goldwater and Faubus, Democrats for Goldwater, and Republicans for Johnson.[12] Rockefeller ran well in the urban counties while Faubus accumulated his majority in the rural ones. Rockefeller ran better than Goldwater in traditionally Republican counties of northwestern Arkansas while Goldwater outpolled Rockefeller in a handful of counties in southern Arkansas.[13] This ability of the Arkansas electorate to split ballots was expressed even more forcefully in 1968 when it picked Wallace for President, Fulbright for senator, and Rockefeller for governor.

The determinants of the low correlation between the Republican presidential and gubernatorial votes in 1964 can be inferred further from the coefficients in Table 17. Compared to Goldwater's vote, the 1964 Rockefeller vote received higher contributions from the traditionally Republican and white collar sectors. In 1966 these contributions plus the contribution of the black belt rose from their levels in the 1964 Rockefeller vote. Especially noteworthy is the very high contribution from the white collar sector in addition to the higher contributions from the other sectors. Thus, the 1966 Rockefeller victory resulted from his improved popularity throughout the state. In 1968 his victory was much narrower, falling from 54 per cent to 51 per cent, when the contributions from each of these sectors declined slightly. In 1970 Governor Rockefeller was defeated by a landslide margin of two to one when the populous white collar sector's contribution to his vote declined precipitously.

A curious feature of Rockefeller's 1966 vote is the high contribution of the black belt, which even exceeded that achieved by Goldwater in 1964.

It would be difficult to believe that this coefficient is measuring Rockefeller's popularity among black belt whites. He cannot be considered this group's candidate from the perspective of either policy or style. His opponent, Jim Johnson, was a staunch segregationist who, it is reported, refused to shake hands with Negroes during the Democratic primary campaign.[14]

Table 18 clearly points to the strong ticket-splitting among black belt whites and Negroes. Goldwater's vote received a strong positive contribution from black belt whites but a negative contribution from Negro registrants; the opposite pattern prevailed in the Rockefeller vote. Unfortunately, voter registration data by race are not available since 1963 but, undoubtedly, Rockefeller received strong Negro support for obvious reasons. Moreover, the size of the Negro electorate has jumped dramatically, an important factor in Rockefeller's victories.[15]

There are several features of Rockefeller's party building efforts which help to account for the course it took but which also point to its ultimate liability. Foremost among these is its personal element; Rockefeller remained aloof from other Republican candidates except those of his own choosing. This was evident in the 1968 election in which Republican businessman-farmer Charles Bernard challenged Senator J. William Fulbright. Bernard, a conservative from eastern Arkansas, waged a campaign similar to Jim Johnson's primary campaign.[16] Rockefeller made certain that the gubernatorial and senatorial campaigns were divorced completely and the regression coefficients point to the radically different bases of the two votes. Moreover, Rockefeller was able to devote the gubernatorial campaign to state issues; national issues did not intrude at all in his campaign in this presidential election year.

The second feature of Rockefeller's party-building effort has been his initiative in appealing to the emerging forces in his state. By contrast, the state's Democratic party, prior to 1970, was one of the most moribund and backward in the South. Faubus, Johnson, and Crank were all characterized as "old-guard" Democrats. Strong white collar support for Rockefeller in three of his four elections was no doubt a reflection of this sector's impatience with the politics of the past. This sector gave strong support to Rockefeller when his was the new face, the change from traditional southern politics. The implication of this formulation for white collar southern Republicanism, however, did not emerge clearly until 1970.

Dale Bumpers was a very dark horse in the Democratic gubernatorial primary. His sole prior political experience had been on his local school board in Charleston, Arkansas.[17] Yet he ran second in the Democratic gubernatorial primary and, although trailing former Governor Orval Faubus by a margin of 156,000 to 85,000, went on to defeat Faubus in the run-off primary.[18] This changed greatly the context of the 1970 gubernatorial election. Suddenly Bumpers was the new face and, in a campaign not marked by great issue differences between himself and Rockefeller, this was a decisive factor. Reg Murphy and Hal Gulliver aptly write that ". . . in Arkansas, as in much of the South, most voters, including those voters who had opted for Wallace in 1968, still tended to vote Democratic. Given an attractive moderate Democratic nominee for governor, a candidate with no scars, the overwhelming majority of the voters preferred that candidate even to a moderate and wealthy and benevolent Republican incumbent governor."[19] In this election the Rockefeller vote fell to 32 per cent and in 1972 Democrat Dale Bumpers went on to re-election by an even greater margin.

Prior to 1970 the question for the new Arkansas Republicanism was whether it could survive without the personal ingredient of Winthrop Rockefeller. And 1970 demonstrated that even Rockefeller Republicanism was an exceedingly fragile phenomenon in Arkansas.

Virginia

It is ironic that it was not until 1969 that Virginia elected its first Republican governor since 1869. For this state has one of the largest traditionally Republican populations in the South and has been a bastion of presidential Republicanism. Presidential Republicanism in Virginia was the product, in large measure, of the indifference, if not covert support, of Senator Harry Byrd, Sr. The passing of his influence, together with the rapid rise in voting participation rates, set the context in which vigorous inter-party competition could take place at the state level. The major consequence of these developments has been the evolution of the state's Democratic party into a much more liberal one than in years past.

In order to seriously challenge Democratic control, Virginia Republicanism has had to depend upon the support of sectors beyond the traditionally Republican base. But this potential additional support has been an inconsistent basis for the vote. In particular, the Negro vote was a Republican resource in the early 1960's, a Democratic resource in 1965 as well as in one of the two U.S. senatorial contests in 1966, and a Republican resource again in 1969.

More clearly than in other southern states, the 1964 Republican presidential campaign in Virginia had a deleterious effect upon the Republican fortunes in subsequent state elections. In 1965 Linwood Holton first ran for governor, facing Democrat Mills Godwin. Holton's 1965 defeat was in large measure a product of the decline in Negro support for the Republican gubernatorial effort since the 1961 election. As Table 17 indicates, the negative contribution of the black belt sector in 1965 was considerably greater than in 1961.

Controlling Negro voter registration, as in Table 18, reveals the dynamics of the shift that occurred here. In both 1961 and 1965 the negative contribution of black belt whites was considerable. Republican gubernatorial candidates could not break the Democratic hold upon black belt whites in southside Virginia, as the Republican presidential candidate had in 1964. But in 1961, Negro voter registration contributed a strong positive increment to the Republican candidate's vote while in 1965 its contribution was virtually nil. This decline in Negro support was a bitter development to Holton, and it was an important factor in his defeat. He had a long record as a racial liberal and had fought the school closing policies of the Byrd organization in the 1950's. To the contrary, his successful opponent, Mills Godwin, had been the architect of "massive resistance" in the Virginia Senate in those years.[20]

The appeal to the Negro vote had been an important element of Republican strategy in Virginia in 1965. Holton tried to build a winning coalition of support in the urban and suburban areas of northern Virginia along with support of Negro voters and the traditionally Republican Virginians. Unfortunately for him, the Democratic nominee also appealed to the first two of these groups. It has been estimated that while 75 per cent of the Negro vote went to Clyde Pearson, the 1961 Republican gubernatorial nominee, only 25 per cent of it went to Holton in 1965.[21] Godwin's success in breaking the Republican hold on the Virginia Negro vote resulted from certain features of the 1964 presidential campaign. In that year Virginia Democrats supported the Democratic national ticket, an unusual stance for Virginia's Democratic party, and Negro voters were grateful. At the same time, these Negro voters distrusted the Republican party for having nominated Goldwater. The Ripon Society writers refer to this disenchantment as "paying the Goldwater debt."[22]

The 1964 stance of Virginia's Democratic party was the result of its rapid evolution to represent the emerging suburban and Negro electorates.

The consequences of this were fully apparent in the 1966 elections. The 1966 Democratic primaries witnessed the defeat of incumbent U.S. Senator A. Willis Robertson and Congressman Howard Smith. Senator Harry Byrd, Jr., newly appointed to replace his ailing father, won renomination only narrowly. Thus, on one hand, younger Virginia Democrats were departing from their party's traditional stance and had engaged positively with the national Democratic party's presidential appeal. On the other hand, the Virginia electorate was repudiating the older stalwarts of the Byrd organization. The twin effects of these developments resulted in a vastly different Democratic party for Virginia.[23]

Population growth and enfranchisement lay behind these changes. The strength of the Byrd organization had been based upon a restricted suffrage and the willingness of rural courthouse politicians to follow the wishes of Senator Harry Byrd, Sr. During the past two decades, Virginia's metropolitan center, which had never been in the forefront of Senator Byrd's concern, grew rapidly in population and needs. The Senator's "pay as you go" spending philosophy was inimical to this rising urban population. The second change which altered the Byrd organization's fortunes was more sudden. In 1964 there was a tremendous expansion of the electorate, following the removal of the poll tax as a prerequisite to voting in federal elections. Undoubtedly, it is this change which prompted Virginia's Democratic politicians to view Senator Byrd's "golden silence" policy in presidential politics as no longer politically practical.

The effects of these changes were also registered in the 1966 general election. Republican James P. Ould opposed William B. Spong, Jr., who had defeated Senator Robertson in the Democratic primary election. Republican Lawrence M. Traylor faced Senator Harry Byrd, Jr. for election to the seat to which Byrd had been appointed following his father's resignation. Spong, who had won his primary victory with the support of Virginia moderates, appealed to these same forces in the general election campaign, while Byrd made very little attempt to gain the support of moderates and Negroes.[24] The regression coefficients in Table 18 reflect these two strategies. Traylor, in the contest with Byrd, received positive support from Negro voters while Ould, in the contest with Spong, did not. Furthermore, estimates indicate that 72 per cent of the Negro voters split their ballots in Virginia in the 1966 senatorial elections and that Spong received 91 per cent of the Negro vote while only 19 per cent of it went to Byrd.[25]

The 1966 senatorial elections in Virginia point up the capacity for change in the Democratic party. It is this party which has been more successful in capturing the winds of change blowing in the Old Dominion. During the 1960's Virginia Republicanism was neither racist nor ideologically conservative. But at the same time it had the advantage of responding to the opportunities which Democratic factionalism presented. In particular, the Democratic factional fight of 1969 set the stage for the historic Republican gubernatorial victory in that year.

The race for the Democratic gubernatorial nomination in 1969 was among three principal candidates—a maverick liberal, a moderate, and a conservative who was considered to be the candidate of the Byrd organization forces. In the run-off primary between the moderate, William Battle, and the liberal, Henry Howell, the state's Democratic establishment supported Battle, who went on to win the nomination.[26] The major consequence of this factionalism was that in the general election Holton benefited from both conservative and liberal Democratic defections.[27] During the general election campaign a "Committee of New Republicans" from the Richmond area, formerly associated with the conservative wing of the Democratic party, endorsed Holton as did the Virginia Crusade For Voters, a liberal group.[28] Whether a majority thus based is durable is open to question.

Further indication that Republican fortunes are dependent upon Democratic factionalism and appeals emerged in the 1970 and 1972 U.S. senatorial elections. In 1970 Republican nominee, Ray Garland, ran a poor third behind Democratic nominee George Rawlings and recently turned Independent Senator Harry Byrd, Jr. In March 1970 Senator Byrd had officially defected from the Democrats and campaigned for re-election to the Senate as an Independent. Despite President Nixon's desire that Virginia Republicans not even offer a candidate against Senator Byrd, Governor Holton was determined that durable Republicanism at the state level depended on the contesting of elections and Garland was nominated. With conservatives rallying to Senator Byrd and liberals to Rawlings, there were very few Virginians available to support the Republican nominee, who polled only 15 per cent of the vote.

A very different outcome prevailed in 1972. As elsewhere in the rim South, this was a very good year for Republican candidates for the U.S. Senate. In Virginia U.S. Representative William L. Scott defeated incumbent U.S. Senator William B. Spong, Jr., the moderate-to-liberal Democrat who had ousted old-guard Democrat A. Willis Robertson six years previous. Two factors account for this historic Republican victory. The climate of opinion in the presidential contest together with the character and appeal of the Democratic opposition provided an unusual Republican opportunity. Essentially, Virginia presented the same situation as North Carolina in the same year. The correlation coefficients indicate that the pattern of the Scott vote had much more in common with the 1964 and 1972 Republican presidential votes than with the 1960 and 1968 ones. And accordingly, the regression coefficients reveal the rural surge quality of the Scott vote as opposed to what has in the past been the more stable but narrow Republican base the white collar and traditionally Republican sectors.

Texas

Inter-party competition was vigorous and persistent throughout the 1960's in Texas. Yet, despite the energy and enterprise of Texas Republicanism, only one candidate, John Tower, has been elected, to date, from the state-wide constituency. Three times, in 1961, 1966, and 1972 he was elected to the U.S. Senate from Texas and is the undisputed star of Texas Republicanism.

Tower first became prominent in Texas politics in 1960 when he waged a strong campaign as the Republican nominee in opposition to U.S. Senator Lyndon B. Johnson. Although this was considered a hopeless task, Tower ran well, no doubt aided by resentment against the Johnson ploy of running for re-election as senator and for the vice-presidency of the United States at the same time. The experience and wide notice of the 1960 campaign was a help to Tower in 1961 when he ran for the seat again when Johnson was compelled to vacate it. Important factors in Tower's 1961 victory were the low rate of voting participation in that year together with the relatively high contribution of the traditionally Republican sector.[29]

Senator Tower was re-elected in 1966 with 57 per cent of the vote while Republican gubernatorial candidate T.E. Kennerly drew only 26 per cent. The explanation of the difference between these two votes lies in the nature of each candidate's opposition, the electoral strategies employed, and the strength of the bases of support for each candidate. Tower's vote was heavily based in the white collar sector, whose contribution exceeded even its 1961 level and also surpassed that of the traditionally Republican sector.

A major factor in the 1966 outcome was the selective deployment of resources. As the star of Texas Republicanism, the retention of Tower's senate seat, following the low Goldwater vote here in 1964 (36.5 per cent), was the chief concern of Texas Republicans. In the 1964 debacle, not only did the Republican presidential vote recede to its lowest level since 1948, but the party lost both its congressional seats and all but one of its state legislative seats.[30] In concentrating on Tower's re-election, the party paid scant attention to challenging popular incumbent Governor John Connally. A corollary of this strategy was that Connally backers were willing to vote Republican for U.S. senator. Tower also benefited from the factional division endemic the Texas Democratic party. His opponent, State Attorney General Waggoner Carr, had been nominated in a bruising primary election which had the result of yielding some liberal Democratic votes to Tower as well in the general election. Thus Tower's 1966 vote benefited from a broad basis of support. The rise in the white collar coefficient together with the rise in the value of the y intercept in 1966 over 1961 reveals this broad popularity.

In winning re-election again in 1972, Tower's vote departed somewhat from its previous character and moved in the same direction as the Nixon presidential vote of 1972, much as had the votes of successful Republican senatorial candidates in North Carolina and Virginia in the same year. The value of the white collar coefficient declined sharply and the value of the y intercept rose sharply for Tower's 1972 vote. This may not be surprising inasmuch as President Nixon strongly endorsed Tower and filmed television campaign commercials with him. The Nixon landslide may have been a factor in helping Tower's re-election in what was anticipated to be a very close election.

Tower's 1972 opponent was Democrat Barefoot Sanders who waged an extremely vigorous campaign and could be classed in the ideological middle of the Texas Democratic spectrum. Sanders was a former White House assistant in the Johnson administration. Tower's potential liability in 1972 resulted from the absence of the advantage he had enjoyed in 1961 and 1966 consequent to the outcome of the Democratic primary elections in those years. For although conservative, he had been supported by some liberal Democrats who were reacting against their party's nominees. One estimate places the size of the Texas liberal Democratic vote at about one-third of the total electorate. The liberal leaders had previously set up organizations to support Tower but were too busy trying to help McGovern take Texas this time.[31] This situation left Tower the option of appealing more directly for conservative and establishment Democratic support. The coalescing of conservative Republican and conservative Democratic forces was symbolically celebrated by the 1973 conversion of former Democratic Governor John Connally into the Republican party.

Although to date only Tower has won election as a Republican from the statewide constituency, inter-party competition has been vigorous in gubernatorial elections as well. Since 1968, Republican gubernatorial candidates have run well, polling 43, 46, and 45 per cent of the vote in the 1968, 1970, and 1972 elections respectively. At the same time, in all of these elections, a strong white collar basis of support persisted for these candidates. Thus, notwithstanding the decline in the value of the white collar coefficient for Tower's 1972 vote, the general trend is for a persistent Republican realignment of the white collar sector on the non-presidential level. Yet, white collar Republicanism is not sufficient for victory in a large and politically heterogeneous state. The Mexican-American community is taking an increasingly active and independent role in the state's politics. In 1972, the gubernatorial candidate of its political party, the Raza Unida, polled more votes than the margin of votes separating the Democratic and Republican gubernatorial nominees.

Florida

Prior to 1964, and again in 1968, presidential Republicanism in Florida was both strong and stable. In 1964, the Republican vote in this state underwent an electoral departure as sharp as that characterized by the deep South. In 1972, a similar electoral departure prevailed again. Prior to 1964, Republicanism was strongest in the populous counties of southern Florida which have attracted so many northern migrants. In 1964, Republican voting strength was concentrated in the rural counties of interior and panhandle Florida which have more in common with their deep South counterparts and which had been strongly Democratic in the past. Thus, two very different patterns have attended Republican voting here.

Both of these electoral patterns have characterized Republican voting on the non-presidential level. Briefly, the election of Claude Kirk to the governorship in 1966 and especially Edward Gurney to the U.S. Senate in 1968 were attended by electoral patterns reminiscent of the Goldwater vote in 1964. Yet, the defeat of Kirk in 1970, as well as the defeat of William Cramer in the senatorial election that year, were attended by patterns of voting more characteristic of the pre-Goldwater vote. Thus, Florida has been the scene of both victory and defeat for Republicanism on the state level but it is only with the Goldwater pattern of voting that Republicans have actually been elected from the state-wide constituency. However, this situation may reflect less the institutionalization of the Goldwater pattern than the character of the Democratic opposition in each of these contests.

In 1966, Florida voters elected their first Republican governor in this century and by a substantial margin at that, 55 per cent. Claude Kirk, a Jacksonville businessman and political opportunist, had campaigned once before throughout the state as the Republican candidate for U.S. senator in 1964. Although Kirk's 1966 vote was positively correlated with all the Republican presidential votes since 1960, it demonstrated a negative value for the white collar regression coefficient. Undoubtedly, it was the continued contribution of the 1940 Republican vote to Kirk's vote which served as a tie between the gubernatorial and the 1960 and 1968 presidential votes, while the values of the black belt and white collar sectors reflected that of the Goldwater vote. Thus, the successful Kirk vote seemed to represent a modest institutionalization of the Goldwater vote.

Tendencies which were modest in 1966 became more pronounced in 1968. Gurney, too, won in a landslide, polling 56 per cent of the ballots, in a vote which was correlated positively only with the 1964 Goldwater vote and the 1972 Nixon one. In this 1968 senatorial vote, the negative contributions of the black belt and white collar sectors which attended the Kirk vote were even greater and there was no contribution at all from the traditionally Republican sector.

In 1970, both the Republican gubernatorial and U.S. senatorial candidates were defeated in votes which clearly resembled the pattern of the 1960 and 68 presidential ones. In the more narrowly confined Republican votes of 1970, the counties which were strongly Republican in 1940 offered the strongest contribution to the Republican vote, a contribution not seen on the non-presidential level since before the 1964 election. A major implication of these contrasting patterns is that in a difficult and losing election year, Republicanism fared best in those counties which had the longest tradition of Republican voting.

From the perspective of the 1970 elections it is clear that the Goldwater pattern of the vote, which did so much to disrupt the previous pattern of Florida Republicanism, had failed institutionalization on the non-presidential level. Yet, in 1966 and 1968 this was not yet apparent. Indeed, quite the contrary pattern seemed to be emergent. Despite the shortlived statistical evidence pointing to the institutionalization of the Goldwater vote in these years, the explanation of the 1966 and 1968 state election votes lies in the nature of the opposition which each candidate faced and in changes in the state's Democratic party. In both years Florida Democrats experienced bruising primary elections in which liberal candidates were nominated. These elections reflected population changes which were sufficient to tip the balance of power away from the conservative Democrats who then did not offer much support to their party's nominees.

In 1966, Florida Democrats denied re-nomination to incumbent Governor Hayden Burns and instead elected as their gubernatorial nominee Miami's Mayor Robert King High, the party's first nominee from "Gold Coast" south Florida. Burns' strength had been in the rural smaller counties of central and northern Florida — the same areas in which Goldwater had run best. Kirk was aware of the potential vote resource in this area and geared his campaign to attracting the support of disappointed Burns backers.[32] Similarly, in 1968, Gurney's opponent, former governor LeRoy Collins, had defeated a conservative opponent in the Democratic senatorial primary election and was viewed as the liberal candidate. Collins also had the liability of his association in several posts with the outgoing Johnson administration.

In 1970, it was the Republicans turn to experience a factional fight as bitter as any the Democrats ever had. Incumbent Governor Kirk was strongly challenged for re-nomination in his own party's primary election and was compelled to face a run-off election. After four years of gubernatorial flamboyance and misgovernment he managed to emerge from the primary season as his party's nominee for a second term, but with so many scars that he was severely handicapped at the general election and polled only 43 per cent of the vote against Reubin Askew, a relatively fresh face in Florida politics.

The factionalism in the Republican senatorial primary was more complex. William Cramer, first elected to the U.S. Congress in 1954 from the St. Petersburg district, was the dean of elected Florida Republicans. He was the obvious and expected Republican candidate for the seat being vacated by Senator Spessard Holland. But Cramer was challenged for his party's nomination by G. Harrold Carswell, the man nominated to the U.S. Supreme Court by President Nixon and rejected by the U.S. Senate. Although Cramer won the primary handily, it is likely that the effects of the machinations behind the Carswell candidacy took their toll in the general election campaign. Carswell was the candidate of Senator Gurney and Governor Kirk who resented Cramer as a rival Republican leader.[33]

In the 1970 elections, Florida's two top Republican candidates presented very different images to the electorate. The *Miami Herald* aptly summarized Kirk's image. "Floridians soon became appalled at Kirk as governor. With no more promise than a lace valentine in the nether regions he went after the vice presidency as running-mate with Nelson Rockefeller, using Republican party funds for this prupose. At home (when he was at home) Kirk set out on a plotted course of confrontation with the Legislature, the news media, the State Cabinet and wherever else he could get a headline. The governorship became a kind of sheikdom lavishly supported by tributes wrung from influence seekers and state suppliers. The result of nearly four years of misgovernment . . . was to leave Kirk's own party embarrassed, Floridians disgusted and the state in an uproar."[34] By contrast, Cramer presented the image of a respectable, conservative, experienced official. It is little wonder, therefore, that despite relatively similar contributions from the traditionally Republican sector for both candidates, Kirk's vote was not supported by the white collar sector while Cramer's was, albeit at a relatively modest level. There is nothing necessary liberal about the white collar sector in southern politics, but it is responsive to good government and reform appeals.

More than any other southern state, Florida expresses on the non-presidential level the two alternative types of Republican voting. In recognition of the distinctiveness of these two types an alternative regression model is presented in Table 19. Here, the 1964 Republican presidential vote is used to predict the 1970 votes in place of the 1940 vote. It thus permits a comparison of the traditionally Republican and Goldwater Republican bases of the vote since 1964. Clearly, the 1964 Republican vote did not contribute to the 1970 votes but the 1940 one did. By contrast, the 1964 Republican vote did contribute positively to the 1966 gubernatorial and 1968 senatorial votes. Apparently, in the long run, the reliable basis for Florida Republicanism is in its pre-1964 pattern. And inasmuch as Cramer polled considerably more votes than Kirk and at the same time enjoyed considerably more support from the white collar sector than did the former governor, it seems reasonable that the pattern of the Cramer vote might well still be the route to Republican victory in Florida. Although a very different electoral pattern was associated with victory in 1966 and 1968, it appears that this had more to do with the character of Democratic factionalism and the Democratic appeal than with a durable basis for Republican development.

TABLE 19

FLORIDA: COMPARING CONTRIBUTIONS OF 1964 and 1940 REPUBLICAN VOTES TO THE KIRK, GURNEY, AND CRAMER VOTES, 1966, 1968, and 1970

Election		a	b_{40}	b_{64}	b_n	b_w	R
Kirk	(1966)	.56	.35	--	-.09	-.13	.53
Kirk	(1966)	.47	--	.18	-.12	.07	.30
Gurney	(1968)	.87	.00	--	-.21	-.54	.50
Gurney	(1968)	.49	--	.62	-.16	-.43	.79
Kirk	(1970)	.24	.63	--	.17	.01	.59
Kirk	(1970)	.30	--	-.02	.08	.31	.20
Cramer	(1970)	.08	.78	--	.04	.39	.79
Cramer	(1970)	.14	--	-.01	-.07	.76	.50

Legend:

a	= Y intercept
b_{40}	= Coefficient of proportion Republican, 1940
b_{64}	= Coefficient of proportion Republican, 1964
b_n	= Coefficient of proportion Negro, 1960
b_w	= Coefficient of proportion white collar, 1960
R	= Multiple correlation coefficient

Conclusion

There is little question but that serious non-presidential Republican competition has become a durable feature of electoral politics, at least some of the time in most southern states. Yet, the quality of this vote appears to be much more variable than its presidential counterpart. On the presidential level the contribution of the black belt was a source of variability while the contribution of the white collar sector was a stable component of the Republican vote, at least aside from the departures in 1964 and 1972 in some of these states. On the non-presidential level the black belt continued to be a source of occasional variability but the white collar sector's contribution itself also became variable both across elections within states and across states. Initially, a major purpose of the analysis of non-presidential southern Republicanism was to examine the effect of alternative patterns of the presidential vote on the gubernatorial and U.S. senatorial votes. An ancillary purpose was to probe the depth of presidential voting patterns. It is clear that the appearance of some non-presidential voting patterns in the mold of the 1964 and 1972 ones supports viewing these presidential vote departures with the utmost seriousness for future southern politics. Yet, in terms of the issue of future state political patterns, the interesting question is less which pattern will be institutionalized but rather what accounts for the increased variability at the state election level.

It is likely that the major reason for this discrepancy between the white collar contribution on the two levels lies in the character of the election contest represented by each election campaign. On the presidential level there is one contest; the meaning of the party battle is read similarly throughout the region and, indeed, the nation as well. But for the state level contests, a different picture emerges. Here the meaning of Republicanism is defined anew in each state and in each campaign. In this process, the character of the Democratic opposition determines in large measure how the voters will respond to Republican candidates. It is not accidental that Rockefeller, Tower, and Callaway were the champions of the white collar sectors of Arkansas, Texas, and Georgia when their opponents represented "old guard" or rural-oriented factions within the Democratic parties. And, it is consistent with this formulation, that Rockefeller's white collar appeal declined precipitously with the emergence of a fresh and moderate Democrat as the opposition in 1970. Similarly, it is not accidental that Kirk, Gurney, Parker, and Ould, in Florida, South Carolina, and Virginia, each received either weak or negative support from the white collar sectors in these states as they faced opponents who were more moderate than they and who did not shun appealing to the urban areas.

Thus, the bases for inter-party competition are more complex and varied on the state level than Senator Goldwater's enthusiasts expected. Voting patterns on the presidential level have the potential for institutionalization on the state level, but this does not occur automatically. At the same time, the alternative bases for non-presidential voting are those expressed on the presidential level. In the period since 1964, the character of the opposition candidate and party had more to do with the fortunes and bases of support for Republican aspirants than did the Senator's candidacy itself. This does not suggest that the 1964 experience was irrelevent; it suggests that the reactions of the state Democratic parties were important intervening variables between the 1964 vote and the subsequent state elections. Virginia provides a case in point.

Part of the fascination of analyzing southern Republicanism is that this was a major new force in southern politics during the 1950's and 1960's which is of major consequence for American politics as well. Change in the American South, however, has not been a one-sided affair. By the end of the 1960's, considerable change in the states' Democratic parties appeared as well. The days when Dixie Republicans could appear to champion the newer emerging forces in society, such as white collar sectors, in battle against backward looking established Democratic organizations are past. Indeed, change may be taking place more rapidly on the state party level than on the national party level. There is now reason to expect that should the state Democratic parties restructure their appeals, the previously almost automatic pattern of white collar Republicanism, as the hallmark of the new southern Republicanism, could be in jeopardy.

FOOTNOTES

1. Gerald M. Pomper, "Classification of Presidential Elections," *Journal of Politics,* XXIX (August, 1967), 535-566.

2. V.O. Key, Jr., *Southern Politics* (New York: Knopf, 1949), p. 75.

3. Some dimension of the unambitious character of Republican leadership in Tennessee is indicated by the fact that in 1966 the Republicans did not offer a candidate for governor. However, it should be noted that this 1966 decision stemmed from the fact that popular former Governor Buford Ellington won decisively in the Democratic primary against a more liberal opponent.

4. John Topping, Jr., John R. Lazarek, and William H. Linder, *Southern Republicanism and the New South* (Cambridge, Mass.: The Ripon Society, 1966), p. 102.

5. Kuykendall was later elected U.S. Representative from the 9th congressional district (Memphis).

6. *Congressional Quarterly Weekly Report,* Vol. 24, No. 40, (1966), p. 2368.

7. For the most complete account of the 1970 elections in Tennessee, see Reg Murphy and Hal Gulliver, *The Southern Strategy* (New York: Charles Scribner's Sons, 1971), pp. 107-130.

8. *Ibid.,* p. 115.

9. *Ibid.,* p. 114.

10. *Ibid.,* p. 123.

11. Topping, *Southern Republicanism,* p. 88.

12. *Ibid.,* p. 41.

13. *Ibid.,* p. 42.

14. Richard E. Yates, "Arkansas: Independent and Unpredictable," in William C. Havard (ed.), *The Changing Politics of the South* (Baton Rouge: Louisiana State University Press, 1972), p. 280. Jim Johnson's wife ran for governor in 1968 and was defeated in the run-off Democratic gubernatorial primary election. Subsequently, she became a leader of the Wallace movement in the state.

15. The size of the Negro voter registration increase has been disputed, but the fact of it has not. One source notes that Negro registration jumped from 73,000 in 1963 to 115,000 in 1966. See William Brink and Louis Harris, *Black and White* (New York: Simon and Schuster, 1966), p. 87. Another source observes that 125,000 Negroes had been

registered since 1964 and that in 1966 there were between 150,000 and 200,000 Negroes registered in the state. See Topping, *Southern Republicanism*, p. 43.

16. Havard, *The Changing Politics of the South*, p. 288.

17. Murphy and Gulliver, *The Southern Strategy*, p. 243.

18. *Ibid.*

19. *Ibid.*, p. 244.

20. Topping, *Southern Republicanism*, p. 122.

21. *Ibid.*, p. 125.

22. *Ibid.*, p. 122.

23. The evolution of the Virginia Democratic Party in recent years has been masterfully chronicled in J. Harvie Wilkinson, III, *Harry Byrd and the Changing Face of Virginia Politics, 1945-1966* (Charlottesville: University of Virginia Press, 1968).

24. *Congressional Quarterly Weekly Report*, Vol. 24, No. 40, (1966), p. 2373.

25. Harris and Brink, *Black and White*, p. 76.

26. It is a measure of the change in Virginia that Howell was elected as an independent in 1971 over Democratic and Republican candidates to fill the vacated lieutenant governorship.

27. Murphy and Gulliver, *The Southern Strategy*, p. 236.

28. *Congressional Quarterly Almanac*, Vol. 15 (1969), p. 1185.

29. The total vote for U.S. senator in Texas in 1961 was 886,091; in 1960 it had been 2,253,784.

30. Topping, *Southern Republicanism*, p. 109.

31. *The New York Times*, October 11, 1972, p. 28.

32. *Congressional Quarterly Weekly Report*, Vol. 24, No. 21, (1966), p. 1090.

33. Murphy and Gulliver, *The Southern Strategy*, p. 148.

34. *Ibid.*, p. 194.

CHAPTER VII

Southern Republicanism and Future American Politics

Concern with competitive elections as the prime mechanism of democratic government, as well as interest in political change, compel attention to the phenomenon of electoral realignment. This involves the study of electoral stability and change, especially the durability of change. Thus, realignment theory is a tool for assessing some of the major changes observed in contemporary politics. In particular, it can be a tool for assessing the voting changes which have swept the South during the past two decades.

The Prospects for Southern Republicanism

The electoral realignment perspective probes for long term similar responses to the parties on the part of the electorate. The persistence of a white collar basis for the Republican vote, especially on the presidential level, is precisely the sort of finding which supports the argument of a durable realignment of this sector. Moreover, this finding is consistent with the class cleavage dimension of the New Deal electoral realignment and the nationalization of cleavages which attend it.

The realignment of this sector and its proclivity to Republicanism augur well for future Republican development in Dixie. For it points to the institutionalization of Republicanism and, thereby, to the development of party. Institutionalization involves the emergence and persistence of organizational structures and cadres as well as durable electoral tendencies. Thus, institutionalization highlights the contribution of realignment to party development.

Institutionalization is also a key concept for the distinction between party and movement. Periods of change and social strain are usually accompanied by popular mobilizations which can assume either a *party* or a *movement* character. The essential difference between the two lies in the institutionalized character of party as compared to the unstable, unpredictable, and less firmly based character of a movement.[1] While it is clear that electoral mobilizations have characterized recent southern politics, their durability have been open to question. That is why the character of

147

the two different patterns of Republican voting, the Goldwater pattern and the white collar dominant one, have been the specific focus of inquiry in this study. One can have greater confidence in the future persistence of an institutionalized pattern than in an uninstitutionalized one. The latter is merely the short term response to the vagaries which come to dominate a given campaign. The unstable voting of the black belt exemplifies such a response; similarly, the massive surge of Nixon support in the South in 1972 is another example.

Notwithstanding its unstable quality, it is well to recognize that the 1972 pattern was not completely unique and that it could recur again at some point. Afterall, the quality of this vote was in the direction cut by the Goldwater swath in 1964. Indeed, the Goldwater vote might yet prove to be the critical election whose potential realignment was held back by the Wallace vote of 1968 which, in turn, became Nixon's in 1972. This would conform to the classic scenario in realignment theory in which a third-party protest vote serves as a half-way house for voters not yet in their new partisan home. Obviously, this would depend upon the absence of serious third-party activity, the persistence of the concerns of race, and a Democratic image of over-sensitivity to these concerns.

The central argument against a new realignment in the mold of the 1964 and 1972 Republican votes lies in the likely non-durable quality of this vote. In both instances the election outcome was in large measure consequent to the nomination of non-centrist candidates for President and the image problems which attended their campaigns. In 1964, the Goldwater appeal was just what many in the white South had been longing to hear; in 1972, the McGovern appeal and constituency were directly opposite what the white South could tolerate. And while the concerns of race were important factors in both years, the diminution and even passing of these concerns in future years could restore electoral cleavages to their more durable mold. [2]

Two measures are used in this probe of recent Republican institutionalization. The first is the pattern of Republican presidential cleavages over time; the second is the emergence of these patterns in the Republican gubernatorial and U.S. senatorial votes. Of course, there are other worthwhile indices of institutionalization, such as competition at the local level as well as the development of a continuing and complex party organizational structure. But it is at the competition for the more visual public offices that new electoral patterns are usually first apparent.

From 1952-1960 and in 1968, the relative persistence of the white collar based Republican voting, to the exclusion of less stable bases, reflects the first measure of institutionalization; the replication of this pattern on most gubernatorial and senatorial votes reflects its second measure. Clearly, the recent development of Republicanism in the South has been a two-step process, occurring first on the presidential and later on the non-presidential levels. Thus, the focus on presidential Republicanism is of immediate and prior concern. This focus can not be stressed too highly. For it was at this level that the first major fissure - the Dixiecrats - appeared in the southern monolith; it was at this level that the Republicans cracked the formerly solid South in 1952.

The two-step diffusion of party competition throughout the South reflects more generally the character of party competition and development in American politics. Of another time, Richard P. McCormick wrote that:

> In the South, as elsewhere, it was the contest for the presidency that exerted the decisive influence on party formation. Parties did not form earlier than 1833 - except in Kentucky - because Jackson was so clearly preferable to his opponents. It was the prospect that Van Buren would succeed Jackson that encouraged opposition elements to form and to contest both state and national elections with those who remained loyal to Jackson's heir.[3]

The twentieth century ascendancy of the Presidency, together with the nationalization of politics, provide ample reason for presidential politics to have an impact on the U.S. senatorial and gubernatorial elections. Moreover, the rapid economic development which has produced the white collar South has yielded a population group relatively free from traditional local political attachments.

Limitations on the Republican Realignment

Because it represents a realignment, Republican prospects in the white collar sector will remain good and predictable. But, outside the white collar sector, Democrats have reason to be sanguine about their prospects. Admittedly, this would depend almost entirely on the diminution of the race issue. There is a current of economic liberalism in the South whose saliency could be to the Democratic advantage. Richard F. Hamilton's analysis of 1964 opinion data reveals that apart from the issues of civil rights and the power of the federal government, there is a reservoir of economic liberalism, especially outside the middle class. In terms of the issues of jobs and medical care, the South, at that time, was as liberal or more liberal than the rest of the population. Of course, whether his finding holds for the late 1960's and the decade of the 1970's is a worthwhile empirical question. Nevertheless, not only is much of the non-white collar and, where appropriate, the non-traditionally Republican South electorally unstable, it has represented a degree of economic liberalism as well.[4]

The Republican liability on economic issues was made manifest by the southern Democratic resurgence in the 1970 elections, providing the first indication in two decades that the overall development of southern Republicanism, beneath the presidential level, need not follow successsive and continuous progress. Although this reflected the southern Democratic party realignment, it was also a measure of the impact of the economic recession of that season which adversely affected Republican candidates outside the South as well. This reflects both the nationalization of politics and the continued saliency of economic class cleavages. In both respects, the meaning of the New Deal electoral alignment is expressed.

Despite the relative dominance of the white collar support for Republican presidential candidates, non-presidential voting patterns do not always reflect this. Both the Goldwater and the pre-Goldwater patterns have been expressed on the non-presidential level. Interestingly enough, in 1972 contests at this level, only one deep South state, South Carolina, presented a Republican voting pattern not strongly or predominantly based on the white collar sector, while in the rim South, three states, North Carolina, Arkansas, and Virginia, did so. Senator Thurmond's 1972 vote stands apart from that of his deep South counterparts. This sub-regional difference reflects the relatively more limited conditions for the institutionalization of non-presidential Republicanism in the deep South, notwithstanding the surge quality of presidential balloting there. Here Democrats still are strong outside the white collar and, where appropriate, the traditionally Republican South.

Despite these variations, the dominant basis for the non-presidential Republican vote has been the traditionally Republican counties together with the high white collar ones. And in this mold, the success of non-presidential Republicanism has been limited, just as the success of presidential Republicanism was limited with practically only the white collar sector as its new base. At the same time, there remain special considerations which affect voting at this level, most notably, the stance of the Democratic opposition. Here as well, victory is more likely to attend a vote more broadly based than in the white collar sector alone.

The limitation which a revitalized Democratic politics places on non-presidential Republicanism points up the emergence of a population sector whose interests diverge from those of the traditional South. But the Republican party is not the consistent and exclusive champion of these new interests. This is precisely the point at which the implications of the present analysis diverge from those of Kevin P. Phillips in his *The Emerging Republican Majority.* Even if the pattern of population growth and economic development continues in the manner which Phillips foresees, this growth need not be a consistent Republican resource. Recent state level elections in Arkansas, Florida, and even to some extent in South Carolina, indicate that new Democratic parties will not always fare badly and that it is folly to presume that only new Republicans will inherit the old Democratic South. The emerging population sectors are looking for an alternative to the traditional Democratic politics of the past, which was often a conservative and rural-oriented politics, and the new Republicanism is not always the answer.

Recognition of these limits of institutionalization also points to the limitations of "southern strategies." The Goldwater southern strategy combined racial and economically conservative themes attractive to the southern white middle class. While this was not without considerable success on the presidential level in the South, it was a strategic failure overall. This is because, aside from certain deep South congressional elections, it had a deleterious effect on the non-presidential contests within the region, as well as on the national electoral outcome. It was a strategy viable in the deep South, but not outside the South at all. Necessarily, the measure of any presidential strategy is its national impact.

President Nixon's southern strategy in the 1968 campaign was considerably more subtle and was targeted more to the rim South, where Republicanism was more firmly established, than to the deep South. His rhetoric of treating southerners no differently than others, as well as his appointment of southerners to prominent positions after his election, were responses to the sense of injury and discrimination which the white South had felt for a long time. From the time of the Civil War defeat to the contemporary period of federal advocacy of civil rights for all Americans, the South felt victimized by the national government. This southern self-consciousness is not unlike the structure of opinion which characterized

George Wallace's northern supporters. In a study of these supporters, Thomas F. Pettigrew, Robert T. Riley, and Reeve D. Vanneman suggested that the psychological mechanism of relative deprivation, the sense of being a member of a group victimized by national neglect, accounted for the Wallace appeal in northern urban areas.⁵ Nixon's advantage over Wallace in appealing to this general attitudinal configuration in the South lies in the presence of institutionalized bases for Republican competition in the traditionally Republican and white collar sectors. Thus, the institutionalization of competition set contextual limits for the successful operation of a southern strategy.

The notion of a southern strategy is less appropriate in accounting for the 1972 election. President Nixon's election strategy in this year was successful precisely because the times, his insight, and the stance of the opposition worked together to allow the formulation of an appeal to which the South and the rest of the nation could repair. This appeal was remarkably similar to Barry Goldwater's in 1964. According to John H. Kessel's account of the 1964 campaign, Goldwater's central themes were a steadfast foreign policy, military preparedness, free enterprise, and law and order.⁶ It would be difficult not to include the place of the Negro in this list as well. In 1964, however, Goldwater was the extremist and President Johnson appropriated the center. In 1972 George McGovern was perceived as the extremist and President Nixon as the center. Of course, the absence of the Wallace candidacy in the general election contributed in no small way to the Nixon landslide. And so in this changed context, notions which were roundly repudiated in 1964 were easily accepted in 1972. There may well be a lesson in this tale for Democratic prospects in 1976.

An exclusively southern strategy is rendered less and less tenable in view of the "southernization" of American politics; the changing character of civil rights concerns—busing for school integration, job discrimination, and welfare—are becoming salient nationally. On election night, 1972, the remarkably similar magnitude of the Nixon landslide in state after state across the nation spoke to the national dimension of the Nixon appeal. With the passing of regional politics, the national integration of the American polity is furthered. This, too, is an outcome consistent with the thrust of the New Deal electoral realignment.

Future American Politics

Three great changes are sweeping American politics—the nationalization of politics, the civil rights revolution, and the on-going trend toward partisan decomposition. A fourth possible and much heralded, but unlikely change, would be the replacement of the New Deal electoral alignment with some new alignment. The development and persistence of competitive southern Republicanism must be appreciated within the context of these existent and possible changes.

The nationalization of politics is a concomitant of the New Deal electoral realignment. During the past two decades inter-party competition has been extended throughout the nation, intruding into pockets of one-party dominance, whether in the South or in upper New England. Political sectionalism, at least as it was once expressed in the South, is antithetical to this trend. One of the important implications of southern Republicanism, in particular white collar southern Republicanism, is that it points to a general convergence of southern and national trends within the context of this national realignment. It is in this sense that white collar southern Republicanism is a mechanism for the integration of the South with the rest of the nation.

It is necessary to recognize, however, that the cause of southern sectionalism is not in total eclipse — the pattern of the Wallace and Goldwater votes expressed it and reflect a transitory divergence between southern and national trends. Moreover, it is plausible to find an expression of southern sectionalism in the dominant Republican realignment itself. Of course this indicates that the vehicle for the expression of southern sectionalism is vastly different today than in previous decades. Realignment in the mold of national electoral cleavages and the continued expression of southern sectionalism need not be inconsistent phenomena. There is every indication that the conservative Republican appeal includes an orchestration of themes, such as opposition to school busing, which non-southerners as well as southerners appreciate. What has happened is that the politics of protest, which was part of the expression of southern sectionalism, has become nation-wide in scope.

During recent decades the issue of race has become more ambiguous than hithertofore and this is why its potential as a realigning issue is diminished. During the era portrayed by Key's *Southern Politics*, the preservation of white supremacy was the primary concern of southern whites. In this simpler era the alternatives on race for the southern white man were easier to comprehend. Democratic loyalty was the crucial mechanism which insured the southern position, while the Republicans were the potential threat to it. Since the U.S. Supreme Court's decision, in 1954, against racial segregation in the public schools, however, it became less clear to southerners where the threat to their interest lay – the Supreme Court, the national Democrats, or the Republican national administration. Civil rights had become less the preserve of one political party as it became national policy, irrespective of which party was in power. And with neither major party unequivocally championing the racist cause, the exclusively racially motivated vote became an unstable one.

The issue of race became ambiguous in another sense as well. The power dimension, which had always been a central consideration in the white supremacy cause, emerged anew with the enfranchisement of the southern Negro. Understandably, the rhetoric of southern politics shifted noticeably between 1960 and 1970 in recognition of the dimensions of the new power configuration. For the "new breed" of Democratic governors, moderation has become as much a prop of power as intransigence was for an earlier generation of office-seekers. Yet the southern Republicans would have difficulty courting the "die-hard" racist vote, which is usually a rural vote, and still retain support in the white collar sector. In addition, the national dominance of the television networks precludes a national political campaign premised on a separate regional appeal. This was one of the lessons of the 1964 Republican campaign.

The third major trend in contemporary American politics – partisan decomposition and disaggregation – has been elaborated into a provocative analysis and argument by Walter Dean Burnham. [7] Briefly, Burnham deals with the declining ability of party to provide a sustained consistent linkage between the citizenry and their governors. This argument is important to consider for any realignment interpretation of recent southern Republicanism because, as Burnham indicates, electoral disaggregation and realignment are incompatible phenomena. Nevertheless, a fascinating hypothesis is that the realignment in southern politics has been possible, in part, because of the very decomposition Burnham disparages. Clearly, southern Republicanism reached a serious level of competition only when ticket-splitting, a prime index of electoral disaggregation, became widespread. The questions which the Burnham thesis presents have yet to be resolved through the experience of American politics of the coming decades.

Given the long-term trend toward electoral disaggregation, two outcomes become possible. One is that the politics of movement rather than the politics of party will come to dominate the political process. In this eventuality, the movement politics of the Wallace campaign and Goldwater Republicanism, which are presently viewed as exceptions to general trends, will then appear to have been harbingers of more usual politics. Indeed, the 1972 election result and voting pattern is an expression of this possibility. However, the rise of movement politics would also mitigate against a possible emerging Republican or any other kind of majority, at least in the sense that past majority alignment eras have existed.

Irrespective of whether the politics of movement or alignment dominates the future, it seems clear that all of American politics will be less predictable, less stable, and less firmly based than hithertofore. In this sense, future elections will assume the character of movement politics in varying degree. This is the case for two reasons in particular. First, the anchor of the solid Democratic south is gone for good, thus removing the last great pocket of reliable residual strength for either major party. Secondly, the increased range of political representation, especially its impact on the primary election level, has made electoral outcomes less predictable from election to election. Quite simply, the smaller the range of groups and concerns a party represents, the greater the degree of control and predictability. Conversely, the greater the range of representation, the less predictable the electoral outcome. In addition there are special problems regarding maintaining the stability and loyalty of the components of heterogeneous political coalitions.

The second outcome of electoral disaggregation lies in the actual persistence of the present alignment era, the New Deal electoral alignment, albeit in a muted form. Past electoral alignments have been noted for their periodicity, for their waxing, waning, and ultimate replacement in a period of three to four decades. Thus, the possible indefinite extension of the New Deal electoral realignment is something new in the history of alignment eras and invites inquiry into its unusual staying power.

Notwithstanding the attenuation of the New Deal alignment in recent decades, the realignment in southern politics may contribute to the reinvigoration of this system of competition nationally and to its persistence. James L. Sundquist has suggested that the New Deal system of competition can be reborn if the activist-conservative opposition regarding the role of government comes to the fore again.[8] Recent southern politics contribute to this outcome inasmuch as Republicanism is a force supportive of the conservative pole while the newer southern Democrats align with the activist forces regarding public policy. One need only consider the different positions of Senators Thurmond and Hollings, both of South Carolina, on the question of rural hunger in their state. Thurmond denied its existence while Hollings was very concerned about the problem. More and more, the forces in southern politics will cleave in a manner consistent with the conservative Republican and liberal Democratic forces outside the South.

The reinvigoration of this alignment may well contribute to the restoration of party as well. The weak and non-responsible character of American political parties has been observed by academic and journalistic commentators alike.[9] One of the implicit concerns of the advocates of responsible political parties two decades ago was the position of and the effects of the South in the Democratic party. Outside the South, the Democratic party had been gradually gaining in strength and in its liberal orientation since 1928. But the innovative thrust of the northern Democrats in Congress as well as in the councils of the party was stymied by the southern Democrats.

This situation is changing, due to increased inter-party competition in the South. There is no question but that the influence of the South, in terms of sheer numbers, in the Democratic congressional party as well as in recent Democratic national conventions is less than it once was. Conversely, the influence of the South in the Republican party and its national convention has increased. Despite the non-routine quality of the Republican vote in 1964, the Goldwater vote was a step in the direction of greater southern influence in Republican presidential politics, due to the incentive method of awarding convention delegate strength. Ironically, the influence of the South in the Democratic party was never less, but this region's influence in the nation, following the Republican presidential victory, was never more.

As the realignment in presidential politics is institutionalized on the non-presidential level, it is likely that the cohesion of the congressional Democrats will rise. At the same time the Democratic presidential platforms and appeals will be directed toward an increasingly liberal constituency while the Republicans will recognize and court their growing conservative one. Party realignment, therefore, follows electoral realignment. Politicians will add to this ideological polarization by switching their allegiances. Conservative Democrats will find the Republican party more congenial just as Thurmond did. Liberal Republicans will become Democrats as John Lindsay did. Party realignment, in turn has its own effects upon the perceptions of the electorate. The events of the 1960's, together with the sharply altered appeals of the Republican presidential campaigns since 1964, have led to a rise in ideological awareness in the electorate which has facilitated such a transformation.[10] And this polarization itself contributes to the persistence of the New Deal alignment.

While, strictly speaking, the New Deal electoral alignment is likely to persist, it is well to recognize two ways in which its manifestation may differ from previous expressions. First, the possibility of a Republican presidential majority is still present. There is no inconsistency between such an outcome and the continued existence of the New Deal electoral alignment. True enough, the consequences may prove different, but the basic underlying phenomenon, the *quality* of the distribution of the vote, would be in the New Deal mold, and the appeals of the parties would remain consistent in a liberal versus conservative opposition. Secondly, the issues upon which politics turns could differ in this stage of the alignment. With the "southernization" of American politics and the changing character of the race issue, this is a distinct possibility. For the concerns of race and economic enhancement are closely intertwined in the nexus of de facto segregation. This fusion may also account for the persistence of the New Deal electoral alignment.

Electoral realignment in the South is a step toward the restoration of party in that it brings partisan appeals into closer accord with the forces in society. The evolving southern Republican and southern Democratic parties thereby provide a broader kind of representation and have fueled a greater voting participation than this region had known hithertofore in this century. But, the very nationalization of cleavages which contributed to the southern realignment is accompanied by problems for the national restoration of party. The maintenance problems of the parties were less severe when they served mainly as sectional spokesmen. On whether a national system of competition and cleavages can represent and contain the conflicts of society rests the course of future American politics. The revolution in southern politics has both altered fundamentally the shape of American politics and yet sustained its recent historic alignment.

FOOTNOTES

1. For an extensive elaboration of the types of mobilizations see Neil J. Smelser, *The Theory of Collective Behavior* (New York: The Free Press, 1963).

2. This is consistent with the argument advanced by James L. Sundquist in *Dynamics of the Party System* (Washington, D.C.: The Brookings Institutions, 1973). More specifically, Sundquist observes that both parties have avoided an exclusively racist appeal. See *Dynamics of the Party System*, p. 358 ff.

3. Richard P. McCormick, *The Second American Party Sysstem: Party Formation in the Jackson Era* (Chapel Hill: University of North Carolina Press, 1966), p. 254.

4. Richard F. Hamilton, *Class and Politics in the United States* (New York: John Wiley, 1972), ch. 7.

5. Thomas F. Pettigrew, Robert T. Riley, and Reeve D. Vanneman, "George Wallace's Constituents," Psychology Today (February, 1972), 477-49, 92.

6. John H. Kessel, *The Goldwater Coalition: Republican Strategies in 1964* (Indianapolis: The Bobbs-Merrill Company, 1968), p. 192.

7. Walter Dean Burnham, *Critical Elections and the Mainsprings of American Politics* (New York: N.W. Norton, 1970).

8. Sundquist, *Dynamics of the Party System*, p. 369.

9. See The American Political Science Association, *Toward A More Responsible Two-Party System* (New York: Rinehart, 1950) as well as David S. Broder, *The Party's Over* (New York: Harper & Row, 1972).

10. For and analysis of the increasing ideological awareness of the electorate, see Gerald M. Pomper, "From Confusion to Clarity: Issues and American Voters, 1956-1968," *The American Political Science Review* LXVI (June, 1972). 415-428.

APPENDIX

MATRICES
OF
VARIABLE PRODUCT MOMENT
INTERCORRELATIONS
BY
STATEa

a - note: All votes are calculated on the basis of the total vote cast, except for 1972 presidential votes, which are calculated on the basis of the two-party vote.

Alabama

	N	WC	P40	P44	P48	P52	P56	P60	S62	P64	S66	G66	P68	S68	P72	S72
N		-.24	-.66	-.69	-.70	.12	-.24	-.17	.40	.37	-.34	-.19	-.60	-.32	-.26	-.38
WC			-.02	-.02	.08	.10	.18	.27	-.05	-.22	.18	.24	.33	.43	-.26	.14
P40				.97	.97	.45	.71	.63	-.18	-.28	.54	.56	.77	.45	.24	.58
P44					.97	.43	.72	.61	-.20	-.31	.55	.53	.74	.42	.21	.52
P48						.43	.71	.64	-.24	-.35	.54	.58	.82	.50	.19	.58
P52							.82	.82	.49	.28	.57	.47	.39	.46	.08	.46
P56								.90	.25	.07	.68	.52	.57	.55	.00	.55
P60									.31	.11	.65	.52	.58	.52	.03	.58
S62										.82	.33	-.12	-.18	.10	.16	.25
P64											.16	-.38	-.37	-.06	.32	.21
S66												.43	.59	.67	.34	.64
G66													.75	.52	-.03	.37
P68														.74	.10	.59
S68															.08	.51
P72																.44

Legend: N-proportion Negro, 1960; WC-proportion white collar, 1960; P-presidential vote; S-senatorial vote; G-gubernatorial vote

Arkansas

	WC	P40	P44	P48	P52	P56	P60	S62	G62	P64	G64	G66	P68	S68	G68	G70	P72	S72	G72
N	-.12	-.72	-.70	-.64	-.56	-.49	-.64	-.26	-.54	.25	-.42	-.04	-.76	-.37	-.07	.49	-.23	-.70	-.43
WC		-.06	.05	.05	.22	.26	.11	.23	.36	.11	.42	.50	.20	-.02	.48	.07	.05	.17	-.12
P40			.94	.91	.83	.76	.82	.50	.72	.06	.57	.34	.86	.60	.33	.05	.28	.64	.70
P44				.90	.88	.81	.82	.48	.73	.06	.58	.36	.86	.59	.36	.05	.20	.65	.65
P48					.87	.79	.79	.55	.79	.11	.60	.41	.87	.65	.40	.16	.24	.65	.66
P52						.91	.87	.65	.79	.23	.64	.57	.87	.66	.57	.23	.33	.54	.65
P56							.80	.69	.79	.31	.63	.56	.81	.69	.54	.23	.34	.58	.58
P60								.58	.72	.09	.64	.55	.91	.69	.60	.19	.41	.51	.72
S62									.70	.59	.46	.44	.54	.61	.45	.23	.49	.26	.44
G62										.18	.82	.60	.79	.61	.61	.22	.26	.67	.60
P64											.06	.13	.07	.32	.21	.32	.49	-.10	.12
G64												.70	.70	.54	.74	.32	.07	.60	.60
G66													.52	.38	.88	.68	.13	.21	.46
P68														.68	.56	.10	.34	.64	.70
S68															.46	.25	.44	.50	.67
G68																.65	.18	.17	.48
G70																	-.04	-.15	.35
P72																		.04	.21
S72																			.50

Legend: N-proportion Negro, 1960; WC-proportion white collar, 1960; P-presidential vote; S-senatorial vote; G-gubernatorial vote

Florida

	N	WC	P40	P44	P48	P52	P56	P60	S62	P64	S64	G64	G66	P68	S68	S70	G70	P72
N		-.46	-.30	-.29	-.29	-.13	-.22	-.21	-.33	-.06	-.28	-.22	-.24	-.33	-.07	-.28	-.02	-.45
WC			.41	.44	.50	.50	.56	.46	.58	-.11	.57	.44	.14	.60	-.40	.50	.18	-.24
P40				.97	.92	.85	.86	.82	.86	-.05	.69	.71	.51	.80	-.13	.76	.57	-.13
P44					.94	.88	.88	.86	.88	-.06	.72	.73	.53	.83	-.16	.80	.61	-.17
P48						.95	.96	.91	.93	-.16	.74	.75	.49	.93	-.30	.87	.68	-.26
P52							.96	.92	.88	-.20	.71	.74	.46	.92	-.36	.87	.72	-.38
P56								.93	.91	-.14	.76	.78	.48	.95	-.33	.89	.69	-.30
P60									.86	-.04	.70	.81	.56	.92	-.17	.88	.73	-.21
S62										-.09	.86	.80	.46	.90	-.28	.86	.59	-.23
P64											.22	.30	.19	-.18	.68	.76	-.04	.56
S64												.86	.35	.76	-.16	.76	.45	-.12
G64													.38	.76	-.07	.74	.51	-.12
G66														.52	.37	.58	.60	.37
P68															-.35	.90	.70	-.25
S68																-.13	.05	.78
S70																	.81	-.11
G70																		-.08

Legend: N-proportion Negro, 1960;   WC-proportion white collar, 1960;
P-presidential vote; S-senatorial vote; G-gubernatorial vote

Georgia

	N	WC	P40	P44	P48	P52	P56	P60	P64	G66	P68	S68	G70	P72	S72
N		-.20	-.33	-.45	-.24	-.39	-.30	.42	.10	-.52	-.20	-.45	-.52		-.22
WC			-.01	-.01	.24	.30	.33	.36	-.03	.50	.48	.52	.50	-.07	.19
P40				.72	.52	.34	.39	.32	-.12	.04	.35	.16	.32	.01	.16
P44					.63	.56	.55	.51	-.09	.04	.44	.24	.34	.10	.20
P48						.64	.75	.57	-.19	.41	.67	.52	.57	-.04	.33
P52							.83	.85	.15	.49	.56	.56	.40	.00	.42
P56								.80	-.14	.47	.69	.48	.54	-.10	.39
P60									.00	.48	.65	.55	.51	.00	.39
P64										.18	-.24	.16	-.21	.21	.22
G66											.50	.65	.45	-.25	.24
P68												.66	.84	.05	.39
S68													.61	.61	.38
G70														-.01	.35
P72															.26

Legend: N-proportion Negro,1960;   WC-proportion white collar, 1960;
P-presidential vote;   S-senatorial vote;   G-gubernatorial vote

Louisiana

	N	WC	P40	P44	P48	P52	P56	P60	S62	P64	G64	P68	P72	G72	S72
N		-.45	-.03	.24	-.10	.18	-.31	.05	.35	.38	.17	-.39	-.68	.01	-.41
WC			.02	.01	.32	.14	.41	.28	.10	-.13	.54	.76	.32	.25	.68
P40				.27	.75	.06	.23	-.12	-.20	-.36	.10	.26	-.16	-.41	.16
P44					.06	.32	.00	.65	.59	.54	.31	.09	.10	.48	-.17
P48						.13	.50	-.11	-.25	-.47	.36	.55	-.14	-.36	.45
P52							.43	.25	.32	.39	.36	.23	.07	.05	.12
P56								.05	-.21	-.27	.28	.52	.22	-.16	.41
P60									.79	.65	.44	.40	.36	.78	.01
S62										.81	.54	.15	.11	.70	-.07
P64											.18	-.12	.25	.74	-.23
G64												.60	-.10	.22	.40
P68													.32	.13	.68
P72														.49	.37
G72															-.01

Legend: N-proportion Negro, 1960;   WC-proportion white collar, 1960;
P-presidential vote;   S-senatorial vote;   G-gubernatorial vote

Mississippi

	N	WC	P40	P44	P48	P52	P56	P60	G63	P64	S66	G67	P68	P72	S72
N		-.36	-.31	-.21	-.24	.40	-.15	.08	-.01	.50	-.08	.35	-.15	-.86	-.17
WC			.50	.33	.44	.42	.68	.51	.41	-.23	.08	.39	.62	.20	.36
P40				.82	.79	.37	.68	.39	.43	-.54	-.07	.23	.45	.10	.01
P44					.62	.37	.51	.44	.42	-.46	-.07	.26	.38	.02	.02
P48						.24	.66	.39	.52	-.64	-.06	.30	.57	.06	-.04
P52							.62	.63	.27	.16	.09	.61	.35	-.49	.16
P56								.59	.45	-.33	.13	.37	.58	-.01	.09
P60									.63	-.16	-.17	.45	.70	-.08	.05
G63										-.36	-.32	.36	.68	.03	-.11
P64											.22	-.08	-.50	-.28	.18
S66												.10	-.16	-.05	.46
G67													.42	-.54	.32
P68														.09	-.03
P72															.05

Legend: N-proportion Negro, 1960;   WC-proportion white collar, 1960;
P-presidential vote;   S-senatorial vote;   G-gubernatorial vote

North Carolina

	N	WC	P40	P44	P48	P52	P56	P60	S62	P64	G64	S66	P68	S68	G68	P72	S72	G72
N		-.15	-.78	-.79	-.83	-.82	-.82	-.87	-.85	-.68	-.76	-.68	-.88	-.84	-.70	-.36	-.35	-.77
WC			-.11	-.09	.03	.16	.19	.16	.12	.15	.20	.03	.18	.07	.09	.18	-.01	.14
P40				.98	.96	.84	.83	.85	.89	.75	.78	.79	.84	.89	.73	.23	.37	.76
P44					.97	.89	.88	.89	.91	.80	.83	.81	.85	.90	.74	.28	.39	.80
P48						.94	.93	.94	.94	.82	.86	.82	.90	.92	.75	.30	.40	.84
P52							.97	.96	.92	.85	.87	.77	.90	.88	.72	.39	.42	.86
P56								.97	.92	.85	.87	.79	.89	.88	.72	.37	.38	.85
P60									.96	.88	.91	.84	.93	.94	.80	.44	.46	.90
S62										.85	.91	.87	.93	.93	.82	.38	.45	.90
P64											.92	.83	.80	.87	.86	.59	.60	.87
G64												.84	.84	.91	.86	.53	.55	.91
S66													.78	.91	.85	.46	.50	.83
P68														.90	.78	.39	.47	.87
S68															.90	.46	.53	.90
G68																.65	.70	.86
P72																	.75	.59
S72																		.62

Legend: N-proportion Negro, 1960;   WC-proportion white collar, 1960;
P-presidential vote;   S-senatorial vote;   G-gubernatorial vote

South Carolina

	N	WC	P40	P44	P48	P52	P56	P60	S62	P64	S66*	S66#	G66	P68	S68	G70	P72	S72
N	-.33	.00	-.25	-.44	.61	-.42	.34	.33	.46	-.38	-.41	.02	-.48	-.58	-.11	-.86	-.72
WC		.33	.33	.50	.22	.58	.43	.42	.18	.21	.31	.27	.61	.33	.35	.21	.23
P40			.62	.45	.24	.31	.16	.10	.10	.01	-.11	.02	.00	.00	-.01	-.07	-.05
P44				.69	.13	.41	.15	.06	-.06	.14	.07	.07	.19	.15	.12	.10	.14
P48					-.03	.60	.11	.09	-.21	.19	.05	.06	.36	.32	.11	.20	.20
P52						.05	.80	.76	.72	.15	.13	.42	.18	-.03	.31	-.47	-.32
P56							.33	.37	.07	.29	.39	.18	.63	.36	.30	.33	.29
P60								.93	.83	.41	.43	.61	.43	.22	.58	-.20	-.02
S62									.83	.44	.44	.64	.43	.24	.56	-.15	-.02
P64										.36	.43	.58	.23	.20	.54	-.14	.06
S66*											.81	.76	.55	.77	.54	.53	.58
S66#												.64	.69	.70	.65	.62	.73
G66													.44	.60	.73	.16	.30
P68														.66	.50	.52	.55
S68															.60	.71	.72
G70																.34	.47
P72																	.91

Legend: N-proportion Negro, 1960;   WC-proportion white collar, 1960;
P-presidential vote;   S-senatorial vote;   G-gubernatorial vote;
*-short term;   #-full term

Tennessee

	N	WC	P40	P44	P48	P52	P56	P60	P64	S64#	S64*	S66	P68	G70	S70	P72	S72
N		.06	-.55	-.54	-.56	-.40	-.51	-.35	-.06	-.07	-.12	-.23	-.49	-.11	-.01	-.13	-.22
WC			-.09	-.12	-.08	-.01	.00	-.06	-.06	-.05	-.02	.10	-.03	.13	.03	.04	.18
P40				.98	.97	.93	.94	.91	.80	.80	.82	.82	.94	.79	.73	.74	.74
P44					.96	.93	.94	.92	.80	.81	.82	.82	.93	.78	.72	.73	.73
P48						.96	.98	.94	.83	.83	.85	.85	.97	.81	.75	.73	.78
P52							.98	.97	.89	.90	.92	.90	.96	.89	.83	.80	.83
P56								.96	.85	.86	.87	.87	.97	.85	.79	.77	.82
P60									.92	.93	.93	.89	.95	.91	.87	.84	.83
P64										.99	.98	.91	.85	.95	.96	.88	.82
S64#											.98	.91	.86	.95	.95	.87	.83
S64*												.92	.88	.95	.93	.88	.85
S66													.89	.93	.88	.86	.87
P68														.86	.79	.78	.84
G70															.97	.91	.89
S70																.92	.82
P72																	.85

Legend: N-proportion Negro, 1960;　WC-proportion white collar, 1960;
P-presidential vote;　S-senatorial vote;　G-gubernatorial vote;
#-full term;　*-short term

Texas

	N	WC	P40	P44	P48	P52	P56	P60	S60	S61	G62	P64	S64	G64	S66	G66	P68	G68	S70	G70	P72	G72	S72
N			.00	-.17	-.28	-.11	-.33	-.02	-.22	-.20	-.19	-.02	-.16	-.07	-.10	-.08	-.42	-.21	-.07	-.07	-.18	.14	-.28
WC				-.07	-.06	.14	.06	.18	.24	.28	.26	.26	.27	.28	.29	.36	.38	.41	.42	.45	.06	.42	.20
P40				.85	.86	.61	.56	.35	.44	.54	.33	.21	.24	.30	.30	.37	.49	.30	.36	.39	.12	.11	.32
P44					.80	.74	.48	.41	.50	.60	.38	.28	.32	.36	.37	.40	.50	.31	.33	.37	.17	.01	.38
P48						.72	.82	.74	.78	.81	.69	.65	.69	.47	.63	.66	.56	.60	.54	.59	.18	.22	.40
P52							.82	.78	.81	.82	.72	.65	.69	.63	.66	.82	.56	.59	.63	.59	.52	.32	.66
P56								.78	.77	.69	.65	.62	.66	.60	.64	.53	.72	.61	.62	.68	.41	.34	.56
P60									.96	.83	.83	.82	.84	.78	.76	.63	.85	.71	.72	.68	.72	.56	.76
S60										.88	.83	.80	.80	.77	.73	.70	.75	.77	.74	.74	.63	.50	.73
S61											.78	.80	.79	.77	.70	.73	.72	.78	.71	.71	.69	.56	.69
G62												.90	.86	.82	.78	.73	.78	.70	.70	.70	.69	.50	.77
P64													.96	.94	.83	.73	.74	.74	.77	.71	.64	.64	.74
S64														.88	.80	.83	.73	.73	.79	.74	.63	.61	.79
G64															.78	.80	.70	.70	.74	.70	.63	.61	.73
S66																.78	.74	.76	.75	.70	.68	.59	.74
G66																	.85	.74	.76	.72	.70	.57	.62
P68																		.69	.75	.72	.50	.54	.78
G68																			.82	.86	.54	.70	.60
S70																				.90	.58	.72	.69
G70																					.49	.69	.62
P72																						.55	.84
G72																							.54

Legend: N-proportion Negro, 1960;　WC-proportion white collar, 1960;
P-presidential vote;　S-senatorial vote;　G-gubernatorial vote

Virginia

	N	WC	P40	P44	P48	P52	P56	P60	G61	P64	S64	G65	S66*	S66#	P68	G69	S70	P72	S72
N		-.33	-.42	-.40	-.45	-.26	-.39	-.41	-.58	.11	-.73	-.77	-.16	-.79	-.75	-.54	-.74	-.48	-.12
WC			-.22	-.22	-.11	.01	.09	.12	.14	-.11	.13	.29	-.07	.09	.29	.24	-.02	.09	-.17
P40				.96	.92	.70	.59	.53	.57	.04	.42	.53	.45	.59	.53	.39	.55	.17	.17
P44					.93	.72	.59	.53	.54	.01	.39	.50	.42	.54	.48	.39	.49	.18	.21
P48						.79	.70	.63	.60	-.01	.44	.57	.49	.62	.58	.47	.54	.21	.17
P52							.73	.69	.33	.21	.15	.35	.26	.37	.47	.42	.20	.31	.27
P56								.80	.61	-.05	.32	.50	.47	.52	.54	.44	.36	.23	.15
P60									.46	.34	.28	.48	.26	.55	.67	.68	.31	.47	.40
G61										-.24	.71	.75	.75	.73	.52	.39	.74	-.02	-.02
P64											-.16	-.12	-.23	.04	.24	.29	-.18	.57	.61
S64												.76	.50	.78	.57	.43	.84	.20	-.06
G65													.52	.86	.72	.62	.78	.28	.00
S66*														.50	.23	.22	.56	-.24	-.14
S66#															.82	.65	.84	.43	.16
P68																.76	.62	.64	.34
G69																	.44	.67	.33
S70																		.17	-.05
P72																			.69

Legend: N-proportion Negro, 1960; WC-proportion white collar, 1960;
P-presidential vote; S-senatorial vote; G-gubernatorial vote;
#-full term; *-short term

SELECTED BIBLIOGRAPHY

Ader, Emile B. "Why The Dixiecrats Failed." *Journal of Politics*. XV (August, 1953), 356-369.

Ader, Emile B. *The Dixiecrat Movement: Its Role in Third Party Politics*. Washington, D.C.: Public Affairs Press, 1955.

American Political Science Association. *Toward A More Responsible Two-Party System*. New York: Rinehart, 1950.

Ashmore, Harry S. *An Epitaph for Dixie*. New York: W.W. Norton, 1957.

Barnett, Marguerite Ross. "Ideological Development in the American Southern Electorate, 1960-1964." Unpublished M.A. Thesis, University of Chicago, 1966.

Bartley, Numan V. *From Thurmond to Wallace: Political Tendencies in Georgia 1948-1968*. Baltimore: The Johns Hopkins Press, 1970.

Barksdale, E.C. "The Power Structure and Southern Gubernatorial Conservatism." *Eassays on Recent Southern Politics*. Edited by Harold M. Hollinsworth. Austin: University of Texas Press, 1970.

Bensman, Joseph and Vidich, Arthur J. *The New American Society: The Revolution of the Middle Class*. Chicago: Quadrangle, 1971.

Berelson, Bernard R.; Lazarsfeld, Paul F.; and McPhee, William N. *Voting*. Chicago: University of Chicago Press, 1954.

Black, Robert Earl. "Southern Governors and the Negro: Race as a Campaign Issue Since 1954." Unpublished Ph.D. Dissertation, Harvard University, 1968.

Brink, William and Harris, Louis. *Black and White*. New York: Simon and Schuster. 1966.

Broder, David S. *The Party's Over*. New York: Harper & Row, 1972.

Burner, David. *The Politics of Provincialism: The Democratic Party in Transition, 1918-1932*. New York: Knopf, 1968.

Burnham, Walter Dean. "The Alabama Senatorial Election of 1962: Return of Inter-Party Competition." *Journal of Politics,* XVI (November, 1964), 798-829.

Burnham, Walter Dean, "The Changing Shape of the American Political Universe." *American Political Science Review,* LIX (March, 1965), 7-28.

Burnham, Walter Dean. *Critical Elections and the Mainsprings of American Politics.* New York: W.W. Norton, 1970.

Burns, James MacGregor. *The Deadlock of Democracy.* Englewood Cliffs, N.J.: Prentice Hall, 1963.

Campbell, Angus; Converse, Philip E.; Miller, Warren E.; and Stokes, Donald E. *The American Voter.* New York: John Wiley & Sons, Inc., 1960.

Campbell, Angus; Converse, Philip E.; Miller, Warren E.; and Stokes, Donald E. *Elections and the Political Order.* New York: John Wiley & Sons, Inc., 1966.

Casdorph, Paul. *A History of the Republican Party in Texas, 1865-1965.* Austin: The Pemberton Press, 1965.

Chambers, William Nisbet and Burnham, Walter Dean, eds. *The American Party Systems: Stages of Political Development.* New York: Oxford University Press, 1967.

Cleghorn, Reese. *Radicalism: Southern Style.* Atlanta: The Southern Regional Council, 1968.

Cosman, Bernard. "Presidential Republicanism in the South, 1960." *Journal of Politics,* XXIV (May, 1962), 303-322.

Cosman, Bernard. "Religion and Race in Louisiana Presidential Politics, 1960." *Southwestern Social Science Quarterly,* XLIII (December, 1962), 235-241.

Cosman, Bernard. "Republicanism in the South: Goldwater's Impact Upon Voting Alignments in Congressional, Gubernatorial, and Senatorial Races." *Southwestern Social Science Quarterly,* XLVIII (June, 1967), 13-23.

Cosman, Bernard. *Five States for Goldwater.* University, Alabama: University of Alabama Press, 1966.

David, Paul T. *Party Strength in the United States 1872-1970.* Charlottesville: University of Virginia Press, 1972.

DeSantis, Vincent P. *Republicans Face the Southern Question-The New Departure Years, 1877-1897.* Baltimore: The Johns Hopkins Press, 1959.

Doherty, H.J., Jr. "Liberal and Conservative Voting Patterns in Florida." *Journal of Politics,* XIV (August, 1952), 403-415.

Eulau, Heinz. *Class and Party in the Eisenhower Years: Class Roles and Perspectives in the 1956 Elections.* New York: The Free Press of Glencoe, 1962.

Frady, Marshall. *Wallace.* New York: Meridian Books, 1966.

Friedel, Frank. *F.D.R. And The South.* Baton Rouge: Louisiana State University Press, 1965.

Gatlin, Douglas S. "Toward a Functionalist Theory of Political Parties: Inter-Party Competition in North Carolina." *Approaches to the Study of Party Organization.* Edited by William J. Crotty. Boston: Allyn and Bacon, 1968.

Grantham, Dewey W., Jr. ed. *The South and the Sectional Heritage.* New York: Harper & Row, 1967.

Hamilton, Richard F. *Class and Politics in the United States.* New York: John Wiley & Sons, Inc., 1972.

Harris, Louis. *Is There a Republican Majority? Political Trends, 1952-1956.* New York: Harper & Bros., 1954.

Havard, William C. ed. *The Changing Politics of the South.* Baton Rouge: Louisiana State University Press, 1972.

Havard, William C. and Beth, Loren P. *The Politics of Misrepresentation: Rural-Urban Conflict in the Florida Legislature.* Baton Rouge: Louisiana State University Press, 1962.

Havard, William C.; Heberle, Rudolph; and Howard, Perry H. *The Louisiana Elections of 1960.* Baton Rouge: Louisiana State University Press, 1963.

Heard, Alexander. *A Two-Party South?* Chapel Hill: The University of North Carolina Press, 1952.

Heard, Alexander and Strong, Donald S. *Southern Primaries and Elections, 1920-1949.* University, Alabama: University of Alabama Press, 1950.

Hero, Alfred O., Jr. *The Southerner and World Affairs.* Baton Rouge: Louisiana State University Press, 1965.

Hess, Stephen and Broder, David S. *The Republican Establishment.* New York: Harper & Row, 1967.

Highsaw, Robert B., ed. *The Deep South in Tansformation.* University, Alabama: University of Alabama Press, 1964.

Howard, L. Vaughan and Deener, David R. *Presidential Politics in Louisiana, 1952.* New Orleans: Tulane University, 1954.

Howard, Perry H. *Political Tendencies in Louisiana 1812-1952.* Baton Rouge: Louisiana State University Press, 1957.

Howard, Perry H. *Political Tendencies in Louisiana.* Revised and Expanded Edition. Baton Rouge: Louisiana State University Press, 1971.

Huntington, Samuel P. "Political Development and Political Decay." *World Politics,* XVII (April, 1965), 386-430.

Jennings, M. Kent and Zeigler, Harmon L. "Class, Party and Race in Four Types of Elections: The Case of Atlanta." *Journal of Politics,* XXI (May, 1959), 198-212.

Jennings, M. Kent and Zeigler, Harmon L. eds. *The Electoral Process.* Englewood Cliffs, N.J.: Prentice Hall, 1966.

Kessel, John H. *The Goldwater Coalition.* Indianapolis: Bobbs-Merrill, 1968.

Key, V.O., Jr. "A Theory of Critical Elections." *Journal of Politics,* XVII (February, 1955), 3-18.

Key, V.O., Jr. "Secular Realignment and the Party System." *Journal of Politics,* XXI (May, 1959), 198-212.

Key, V.O., Jr. *Politics, Parties and Pressure Groups.* Fifth Edition. New York: Thomas Y. Crowell, 1964.

Key, V.O., Jr. *Southern Politics.* New York: Knopf, 1949.

Key, V.O., Jr. and Munger, Frank. "Social Determinism and Electoral Decision: The Case of Indiana." *American Voting Behavior.* Edited by Eugene Burdick and Arthur J. Brodbeck. New York: The Free Press, 1959.

Kirkpatrick, Evron M. "Toward a More Responsible Two-Party System: Political Science, Policy Science, or Pseudo-Science?" *The American Political Science Review,* LXV (December, 1971), 965-990.

Ladd, Everett Carll. *American Political Parties.* New York: W.W. Norton, 1970.

Lerche, Charles O., Jr. *The Uncertain South: Its Changing Patterns of Politics in Foreign Policy.* Chicago: Quadrangle Books, 1964.

Lowi, Theodore J. "Toward Functionalism in Political Science: The Case of Innovation in Party Systems." *American Political Science Review,* LVII (September, 1963), 570-583.

Lowi, Theodore J. *The Politics of Disorder.* New York: Basic Books, 1971.

Lubell, Samuel. *The Future of American Politics.* Third Edition, Revised. New York: Harper & Row, 1965.

MacRae, Duncan, Jr. "Occupations and the Congressional Vote 1940-1950." *American Sociological Review.* XX (June, 1955), 332-340.

MacRae, Duncan, Jr. and Meldrum, James A. "Critical Elections in Illinois: 1888-1958." *American Political Science Review,* LIV (September, 1960), 669-683.

McCormick, Richard P. *The Second American Party System: Party Formation in the Jacksonian Era.* Chapel Hill: The University of North Carolina Press, 1966.

McGill, Ralph. *The South and the Southerner.* Boston: Little, Brown and Company, 1959.

McKinney, John C. and Bourque, Linda B. "The Changing South: National Incorporation of a Region." *American Sociological Review,* XXXVI (June, 1971), 399-412.

McKinney, John, ed. *The South in Continuity and Change.* Durham: Duke University Press, 1965.

Murphy, Reg and Gulliver, Hal. *The Southern Strategy.* New York: Scribner's 1971.

Matthews, Donald R. and Prothro, James W. *Negroes and the New Southern Politics.* New York: Harcourt, Brace and World, 1966.

Nicholls, William H. *Southern Tradition and Regional Progress.* Chapel Hill: University of North Carolina Press, 1960.

Novak, Robert D. *The Agony of the G.O.P. 1964.* New York: MacMillan Company, 1965.

Patterson, James T. *Congressional Conservatism and the New Deal: The Growth of the Conservative Coalition in Congress, 1933-1939.* Lexington, Ky.: University of Kentucky Press, 1967.

Pettigrew, Thomas F. and Campbell, Ernest Q. "Faubus and Segregation: An Analysis of Arkansas Voting." *Public Opinion Quarterly,* XXIV (Fall, 1960).

Pettigrew, Thomas F.; Riley, Robert T.; and Vanneman, Reeve D.; "George Wallace's Constituents." *Psychology Today,* February, 1972, pp. 47-49, 92.

Phillips, Kevin P. *The Emerging Republican Majority.* New Rochelle, N.Y.: Arlington House, 1969.

Pomper, Gerald M. "Classification of Presidential Elections." *Journal of Politics,* XXIX (August, 1967), 535-566.

Pomper, Gerald M. "From Confusion to Clarity: Issues and American Voters, 1956-1968." *American Political Science Review,* LXVI (June, 1972), 415-428.

Pool, Ithiel de Sola; Abelson, Robert P.; and Popkin, Samuel L. *Candidates, Issues and Strategies: A Computer Simulation of the 1960 and 1964 Presidential Elections.* Cambridge, Mass.: The M.I.T. Press, 1965.

Price, Hugh Douglas. "The Negro and Florida Politics, 1944-1954." *Journal of Politics,* XVII (May, 1955), 198-220.

Price, Hugh Douglas. *The Negro and Southern Politics: A Chapter of Florida History.* New York: Harcourt, Brace & World, 1966.

Price, Douglas, "Micro- and Macro-politics: Notes on Research Strategy." *Political Research and Political Theory.* Edited by Oliver Garceau. Cambridge, Mass.: Harvard University Press, 1968.

Prothro, James W. "Two-Party Voting in the South: Class vs. Party Identification." *American Political Science Review,* LII (March, 1958), 131-139.

Rusher, William A. "Crossroads for the G.O.P." *National Review, February 12, 1963, pp. 109-112.*

Scammon, Richard M. and Wattenberg, Ben J. *The Real Majority.* New York: Coward-McCann, 1970.

Schattschneider, E.E. "United States: The Functional Approach to Party Government." *Modern Political Parties.* Edited by Sigmund Neumann. Chicago: University of Chicago Press, 1956.

Seagull, Louis M. "The Youth Vote and Change in American Politics." *The Annals,* 397 (September, 1971), 88-96.

Shannon, Jasper. *Towards a New Politics in the South.* Knoxville: The University of Tennessee Press, 1949.

Sherrill, Robert. *Gothic Politics in the Deep South.* New York: Grossman, 1968.

Sindler, Allan P. "Bifactional Rivalry As An Alternative To Two-Party Competition in Louisiana." *American Political Science Review,* XLIX (September, 1955), 641-662.

Sindler, Allan P., ed. *Change in the Contemporary South.* Durham: Duke University Press, 1963.

Sindler, Allan P. *Huey Long's Louisiana: State Politics, 1920-1952.* Baltimore: Johns Hopkins University Press, 1956.

Smelser, Neil J. *The Theory of Collective Behavior.* New York: The Free Press, 1963.

Soukup, James R.; McCleskey, Clifton; and Holloway, Harry. *Party and Factional Division in Texas.* Austin: University of Texas Press, 1964.

Strong, Donald S. "The Presidential Election in the South, 1952." *Journal of Politics,* XVII (August, 1955). 343-389.

Strong, Donald S. *Urban Republicanism in the South.* University, Alabama: University of Alabama Press, 1960.

Sundquist, James L. *Dynamics of the Party System.* Washington, D.C.: The Brookings Institution, 1973.

Tindall, George Brown. *The Disruption of the Solid South.* Athens: University of Georgia Press, 1972.

Topping, John C., Jr.; Lazarek, John R.; and Linder, William H.; *Southern Republicanism and the New South.* Cambridge, Mass.: Republicans for Progress and the Ripon Society, 1966.

U.S. Commission on Civil Rights. *Report: Voting 1960.* Washington, D.C.: Government Printing Office, 1961.

Vines, Kenneth N. *Republicanism in New Orleans.* New Orleans: Tulane University Press, 1955.

Vines, Kenneth N. *Two Parties for Shreveport.* Case Studies in Eagleton Foundation Series. New York: Holt, 1959.

Viorst, Milton. *Fall From Grace: The Republican Party and the Puritan Ethic.* New York: The New American Library, 1968.

Watters, Pat. *The South and the Nation.* New York: Pantheon Books, 1969.

Watters, Pat and Cleghorn, Reese. *Climbing Jacob's Ladder: The Arrival of Negroes in Southern Politics.* New York: Harcourt, Brace and World, 1967.

Weeks, O. Douglas. *Texas In The 1960 Presidential Election.* Austin: University of Texas-Bureau of Government, 1961.

Wicker, Tom. "George Wallace: A Gross and Simple Heart." *Harper's Magazine, April, 1967, pp 41-49*

Weltner, Charles L. *Southerner.* Philadelphia: J.B. Lippincott, 1966.

White, T.H. *The Making of the President, 1968.* New York: Atheneum, 1969.

White, T.H. *The Making of the President, 1972*. New York: Atheneum, 1973.

Wilkinson, J. Harvie, III. *Harry Byrd and the Changing Face of Virginia Politics, 1945-1966*. Charlottesville: University of Virginia Press, 1968.

Woodward, C. Vann. *The Burden of Southern History*. Revised ed. Baton Rouge: Louisiana State University Press, 1968.

INDEX